Screamin' Leeman's Movie Reviews
The Good, The Bad, and The Putrid

By Bill Leeman

For Carol

I would like to dedicate this book to my loving wife and best friend Carol Butler, who has been a constant source of encouragement, inspiration, love, joy and laughter since the day we met thirty years ago.

Hey, remember Casablanca? Well, that's not reviewed here. But Cabin In The Woods is, which is one of the great sci-fi horror films of all time. And so is This Is The End, the coolest end-of-the-world film you'd ever want to see. And so is Killer Joe, the best film that Quentin Tarantino had nothing to do with.

And along with those are a bunch of so-called great movies, which are really dogs — such as The Irishman, House Of Gucci, and LaLa Land.

Not to mention some fabulous documentaries such as Free Solo, The Wolfpack, and Rodents Of Unusual Size.

Maybe you forgot about some of these movies. Maybe you missed some of them completely. Maybe your favorite movie is on this list.

This book can serve as a reminder to see those ones you might have missed, or see the ones you loved once again.

For myself, when I was compiling the list, I realized I had forgotten about Killer Joe (OMG). So I rented it on Netflix and got to experience that brilliant piece of work all over again.

Now, you may not agree with my picks, and which films are dogs, and which ones are great. But that's okay.

Just remember: One man's soap is another man's soup.

Movie Categories

Just reading the titles of some of these movies will take you back, and remind you how much you hated them (Or loved them). Our reviewer has certain opinions. See if you agree.

Comedies	**(Com)**
Dramas.	**(Dra)**
Science Fiction	**(Sci-Fi)**
Horror.	**(Hor)**
Musicals	**(Mus)**
Documentaries	**(Doc)**
War	**(War)**
Foreign Film	**(FF)**
Fantasy	**(Fan)**

Ratings

Brilliant Piece Of Work	**(BPOW)**
Most Excellent Movie	**(MEM)**
Highly Recommended	**(HR)**
Remarkable	**(Re)**
Wonderful Heart-wrenching Movie	**(WHWM)**
Fascinating Movie	**(FM)**
Interesting Movie	**(IM)**
Very Interesting Movie	**(VIM)**
Very Entertaining	**(VE)**
I Hated It	**(IHI)**
Good Movie	**(GM)**
Very Good Movie	**(VG)**
Good, But Tough To Watch.	**(TTW)**
Unintentionally Laughable	**(UL)**
BORING With A Capital B	**(BCB)**
Just Plain Stupid	**(JPS)**

Stay Away	(SA)
Avoid Like The Plague	(AVLP)
Boring or Tedious	(Bor-T)
Sure Cure For Insomnia	(Snore)
Clunker/Stinker	(PU)
I'll Never Get That Time Back	(INGTTB)
Embarrassment	(Emb)
What's The Point?	(WTF)
Moronic	(M)
Sappy, but Okay	(SapO)
No One Gives A Rat's Ass	(NOGARA)
Don't Waste Your Time	(DWYT)
One Good Scene	(OGS)
Overdone, Too Long	(OTL)

For Very Discerning Tastes
(You Know Who You Are)   (VDT-YKW)

Movie So Crappy It Makes You Angry
As In: *This one really pissed me off*   (TORPMO)

Movies That Are A Turn-off Because
Of Actions By the Actor, In Other Words,
You Really Screwed That One Up   (YRSTOU)

Movies That Paled In Comparison To
Other Things Going On In And Around
The Theater   (WOW)

INDEX

Magic Mike.....................Dra........................WOW
This Is The End................Com, Dra,.............BPOW
Saving Mr. Banks.............Dra.......................WTF
Lone Survivor.................War.......................IM
The Oath.....................Com, Dra.................HR
Babylon......................Com.......................OTL
Rodents Of Unusual Size...Doc.......................FM
Free Solo.....................Doc....................FM, HR
Crazy Rich Asians...........Dra.......................INGTTB
Rock Of Ages................Com, Mus..............IM, Bor-T
Shoplifters..................FF, Dra...................IM
Vice.........................Dra, Com...............IM
Bohemian Rhapsody........Mus, Dra...............IM
Wayne's World...............Com..............MEM, HR
The Wedding Guest.........Dra.......................PU
Get Out.......................Sci-Fi, Hor..............HR
Us............................Hor.......................INGTTB
At Eternity's Gate.............Dra..........PU, Snore, INGTTB
Deconstructing The Beatles..Doc..Bor-T, PU, WTF, INGTTB
Linda Ronstadt: The Sound Of My Voice...Doc..BPOW, HR
Judy..........................Dra.......................Bor-T, PU
The Irishman.................Dra.......................Emb
A Marriage Story.............Dra.......................IM
Joker.........................Dra.......................MEM, HR
A Beautiful Day In The Neighborhood...Doc........WHWM
Once Upon A Time In Hollywood...Dra...............GM
Jumanji: The Next Level...Com, Dra....PU, Emb, INGTTB
Knives Out...................Dra.......................Bor-T
Rocketman..................Mus.......................GM
Bombshell...................Dra.......................GM
Richard Jewell..............Dra.......................?
Parasite......................Dra.......................IM, FM

Motherless Brooklyn.......Dra..............................Emb
Hustlers.......................Dra….......PU, E, WTF, INGTTB
Uncut Gems…...............Dra….........................IM
Jojo Rabbit.....................Dra, Com…............…...Snore
The Good Liar……...….....Dra…...........…........…IM
Where's My Roy Cohn?...Doc.........................…MEM, HR, FM
David Crosby: Remember My Name….Doc…....Bor-T
Little Women..Dra……You didn't really think I'd see this, Did you?
Downhill......................Dra….......................MEM
The Cabin In The Woods…Hor.....................…..BPOW, HR
Tiny Tim: King For A Day…Doc…........…...........MEM
Trial Of The Chicago 7…….Dra…...................…HR
Nomadland....................Dra, Doc….................Emb, WTF
The Adjustment Bureau……Dra….....................PU, INGTTB
Don't Look Up....................Com, Dra…...........MEM, HR
West Side Story…............…Mus…...............….MEM, HR
House Of Gucci……............Dra…..................…PU, Emb, WTF
Nobody….......................…Dra…....................MEM, HR
The Shape Of Water….........Dra….........…...........UL
San Andreas....................Dra…....................WOW
Glen Campbell, I'll Be Me…Doc, Mus…...........WHWM, HR
Licorice Pizza......................Dra….......…..........SapO
Scream..........................Hor….....................OGS
Jackass........................Com, Doc….........…......Emb!!
Coda…............................Dra…..........................Bor-T
Nightmare Alley…….............Dra….......................Bor-T
Belfast,,,,,,,,,,,,,,,,,,,,,,----…...,,,Dra….............
King Richard.....................Dra.....................YSTOU
Dune……............Sci-Fi…......Is this one as boring as the first one?
Drive My Car…...............FF.............................NOGARA
The Power Of The Dog……..Dra.......................MEM
Elvis….............................Dra.......................MEM
Triangle Of Sadness….........Dra…...................…VIM, HR
Babylon…........................Dra…..................…Bor-T
Django, Unchained….........Dra…...................…MEM, OTL
Argo…........................Dra..........................SA

Barbarian.........................Hor.........................MEM, HR
The Armstrong Lie.............Doc........................MEM, HR
Muscle Shoals............Mus, Doc...............MEM!!, HR!!
Blue Is The Warmest Color.....FF, Dra............MEM, HR
The Wolf Of Wall Street...........Dra..................SA
Bad Grandpa....................Com...................VG, HR!!
Inside Llewyn Davis............Dra.....................IHI
Her.............................Sci-Fi......................Bor-T, IHI
The Equalizer...............Dra..........................JPS
Birdman, Or The Unexpected Virtue Of Ignorance..Dra..IHI
Gone Girl......................Dra...........................IM
The Girl Who Walked Home Alone At Night..FF, Dra...Snore
Wolfpack..................Doc............................FM, MEM, HR
Jurassic Park...........Sci-Fi, Dra....................Bor-T
Deadpool..............Com.................................BPOW
Deadpool 2...........Com.................................BPOW
Hereditary......................Hor.........................DWYT
Won't You Be My Neighbor....Doc...................WHWM
Battle Of The Sexes..............Dra...........Bor-T, INGTTB
LaLa Land..........................Mus.....................IHI
I, Tonya.............................Dra........................TTW
All The Money In The World...Dra....................INGTTB
Silence............................Dra........................Bor-T
Don Jon..............................Dra......................MEM, HR
The Disaster Artist.............Dra.....................TORPMO
Where To Invade Next........Doc...............VE, MEM, HR
The Big Short.....................Doc........................MEM
The Hateful Eight...............Dra........................GM
Shtar Warsh, Inshtallment Sheven
(The Forshe Awakensh).........Fan...............NOGARA, SA
The Revenant.......................Dra...........OGS, TORPMO
Brooklyn.............................Dra................MEM, HR
Point Break.......................Dra.......Emb, WTF, JPS, SA,
Arrival................................Sci-Fi....…..….....BCB, JPS, SA
August: Osage County......,,,.Dra.............Re, BPOW, HR
The Counselor....................Dra.........TORPMO, JPS, SA

Gravity.....................................Dra….........................M, SA
Awake, The Life Of Yogananda…Doc…....................Snore
Wild Tales…......................…Dra…....…..BPOW, MEM, HR
The Walk…......................…Dra…........................MEM, HR
Invasion Of The Body Snatchers 1956…Sci-Fi….MEM, HR
Invasion Of The Body Snatchers 1978…Sci-Fi….MEM, HR
All Austin Powers Films…..Com......................(VDT-YKW)
<u>SISU</u> ....…..Dra.....................(VDT-YKW)

Magic Mike

Starring Matthew McConaughey and others

Took the little woman to the movies the other night. But now that I think about it, it seems like she took me. Yes. Went to see "Magic Mike," starring Matthew McHunky and some other dudes. You know, I didn't have any idea that I was this naive. I guess I am, though.

You know what it's about, don't you? Its about a few guys who are male strippers. That's it. No story needed, no plot, no theme, no dialogue necessary. It's all about these guys baring their manly chests, flexing their abs, showing a little bun, and bumping and grinding and groping all these excited women.

That's what I mean about being naive. I had no idea. Anyway, we sat down, the movie started, and for the first ten or fifteen minutes, I thought to myself, "Hey, this might be pretty good!" But at the sixteenth minute, I realized: Nope, this is all there is. It definitely is not going to get any better.

Now, sitting in a movie theater, being bored, my eyes and my mind always begin to wander. As my mind was wondering how I could get out of there without creating a scene, my eyes began to look around at the audience, and I noticed that the entire theater was filled with women. And I mean FILLED, and I mean ALL women. And judging from the squeals and shrieks going on, they were enjoying it quite a bit more than I was. As a matter of fact, when the darned thing was over, very few of them left their seats.

My guess: They were spent.

There they sat, women of all ages, every nationality and race (there was no way to check religions, but I'm sure they were all represented); women of every stripe, all in quite the frenzied little dither over Matthew McWhatever and his pecs, abs, and buns.

In order to get out, I had to climb over what appeared to be a family; a grandma, a mom, and a daughter, who were all sweaty and panting.

I ambled out to the hallway to watch as the women slowly left the theater.
It was like a bunch of teenage girls after a heavy make-out session. All these
gals, in all states of disarray, hair messed up, clothes damp and wrinkled,
unmistakable signs of drool on their blouses; all of them with looks on their faces
that seemed to say, *"Ooh, I was bad, and it was good..."*

I highly recommend this movie to women of all ages who would like a little
titillation, or maybe some fodder for their imaginations.

Guys: Stay home. Watch the ball game.

This Is The End

Starring

Seth Rogan	as	Seth Rogan
Jay Baruchel	as	Jay Baruchel
Jonah Hill	as	Jonah Hill
James Franco	as	James Franco
Craig Robinson	as	Craig Robinson
Danny McBride	as	Danny McBride
Emma Watson	as	Emma Watson
Rihanna	as	Rihanna

Etcetera, etcetera, etcetera..

Now, we are all familiar with 'chick flicks.' You know, movies that are sappy, or syrupy, or that have an emotional story line and no explosions. Well, what about 'guy flicks?' How come we never hear about them? Is anything that is *not* a chick flick a guy flick? Never mind, it's a rhetorical question.

The reason I bring it up is because you would have to define this one as a 'guy' flick for sure. Not that women couldn't enjoy it, as a matter of fact there were several women in my vicinity having a great old time, not to mention that accompanying me were my lovely daughter and my distinguished niece, and they both loved it.

As much mayhem, profanity, and general distastefulness that this movie employs, it is done, or should I say overdone, in a classy way. Now, it's been a lot of years since I stood at the hash pipe, but I'm telling you, this would be a *perfect* movie to go to stoned. But it is great, stoned or not.

Some of the other reviewers were saying *"It's really funny,"* but I always take that with a grain of salt. One man's very funny is another man's vomitorium, I always say. But I figured, okay, we could get lucky, and have a few laughs. Let me tell you, this one was TEN TIMES as good as I thought it would be.

Nothing but good, clean, fun! Well, maybe not that clean. As a matter of fact, it is
filthy. But it is also very funny. And crazy. And hilarious. At first I thought it was
going to be just another pot-smoking wing job, but I was wrong about that.

The story line is this: It starts out as a Hollywood party with a bunch of movie
stars getting stoned and chillin' when all of a sudden: The Apocalypse is upon us!
Mayhem! Pandemonium, bedlam and havoc! And when the maelstrom starts, it
starts GOOD! Earth breaking, walls cracking, sinkholes opening, fire, brimstone,
and monsters. In a few short moments, the LA party becomes a panic-stricken
hell-on-earth. But a really *funny* panic-stricken hell-on-earth.

Our cast ends up trapped in James Franco's mansion trying to figure out what's
happening and what to do. Now, facing the end of the world, their different
personalities begin to emerge. I won't spoil it, suffice to say it only gets better from
there.

This thing alternates between scaring the bejesus out of you, and making you
laugh your butt off. There are very funny moments, and very scary moments. As
a matter of fact, I, myself, screamed OUT LOUD no less than four times. But no
one heard my screams because they were all screaming as well.

The whole thing boils down to one heck of a lot of fun!

   AND, if you want to look at it from another point of view, the psychological
implications of certain monsters chasing certain people are, well, fitting. Talk about
your weird, Freudian nightmares...

And that's another great thing about this movie. *Character development.* What a
concept! Although they are all playing themselves, all the facets of each unique
personality are developed. Some we like, some we don't, but we can relate to all
of them as real people.

Very funny, very good, and it ends on a high note.

The three of us were laughing and talking about it all the way home, and into the
house.

I highly recommend it. Highly.

Saving Mr. Banks and Lone Survivor

Emma Thompson
Tom Hanks
Paul Giamatti
Lone Survivor
Mark Wahlberg

Lone Survivor is the gut-wrenching true story of a group of Navy Seals (who, as we know, are the baddest of the bad) who go into Afghanistan on a mission and end up in a fire fight where they all die. Except for one, of course, hence the title.

Saving Mr. Banks is the gut-wrenching true story of P. L. Travers, the author of Mary Poppins who, because of her sordid childhood, turned out to be probably the biggest pain-in-the-ass ever to set foot on American soil. Now, I have never had much use for *anything* Disney, let alone Mary Poppins, but a couple of people recommended this one as something to see.

(Hopefully, I can find a way to return the favor).

I will say this: Emma Thompson does a first-rate job playing the part of Travers, who comes across as a contemptuous, overbearing, snob of the highest degree. I *hated* her character.

Now, some people, who are a little more in touch with the Freudian side of things, might say I'm *projecting.*

In any case, this whole movie was so squeaky clean it *felt* like we were in Disneyland. I was ready to puke.

Lone Survivor

So, in order to get the sickeningly sweet and syrupy taste out of my mouth, I had to go to the opposite extreme. Consequently, I checked out Lone Survivor.

While the credits were rolling at the end of the film, they showed real-life pictures of all the guys that had died. Pictures with their girlfriends, at their weddings, with their little kids, etc. Very sad.

And I couldn't help but think: Dying on some god-forsaken mountain in Afghanistan? What a waste.

But this is about our gender more than anything. There is a little Navy Seal in all of us (men, that is). I mean, that's why we can relate, because somewhere hidden deep inside all of us, we want to be those guys. The toughest of the tough, the baddest of the bad. It's in our genes. That's why guys get in fights all the time. Why do you think there is football? Rugby, soccer? Most sports, for that matter. Because of the testosterone! It comes with the territory. Mother Nature put it there to keep the species going.

Look at the history of humankind: Now, let's see, the men all run around creating havoc, squabbling, fighting, trying to prove who's the strongest, all of which eventually lead to war, while the women of the species give birth and nurture.

But all this is a whole different story, way too long and involved to be told here.

Anyway, what's the point?

Is anything going to change?

The Oath

Ike Barinholtz
Tiffany Haddish
John Cho

Okay, this one is really something.

What starts out as a seemingly light-hearted comedy about the differences in families with regard to politics and political leanings over a Thanksgiving dinner gets darker and more volatile with each passing minute and each passing insult.

Set in Anytown, USA, a family is getting ready for Thanksgiving and discussing the new "Oath" that has been prescribed by the President swearing allegiance to him, and that all citizens are advised to sign. There are no penalties for not signing, but it is implied that there may be perks for those who sign, and for those who don't… who knows?

As you can imagine, this stirs up quite a fierce debate between liberals and conservatives, especially in the same families, as depicted in this film.

As the deadline to sign approaches (Black Friday, the day after Thanksgiving), people's nerves start to drive them to distraction.

The Thanksgiving dinner is being held in the movie's hot-headed liberal news junkie's house and when his conservative brother and his girlfriend arrive, and the subject of The Oath comes up, the 'S' really starts to hit the 'F'. Which is bad enough, but then a couple of government agents show up, and the whole thing goes completely over the top.

And what started out as (what we thought) was going to be a light comedy becomes something quite different.

Not a dull moment in this one, folks. Very well done, despite a few discrepancies, but let's not nit-pick.

Reminds one a lot of what is happening in this country today.

I'd like to see it again.

Therefore, I highly recommend it.

Rodents of Unusual Size

A Documentary by Quinn Costello, Chris Metzler & Jeff Springer

I just came from seeing an amazing documentary about giant rodents that are eating Louisiana.

Sounds like a corny science fiction flick, does it not?

Except that it is true.

"Rodents of Unusual Size" tells the story of these huge rat-like creatures, called Nutria, who can weigh upwards of 20 pounds, have voracious appetites, and reproduce like bunnies.

Nutria. Sounds like a healthy food drink, doesn't it?

I can assure you it is not. These things look like giant hunch-backed rats with webbed feet and large, long, rat-like tails.

They are not native to North America and they have no known natural predators. With their orange eyes and giant orange teeth, they look like a cross between an enormous woodchuck and a deformed beaver in a halloween mask.

They have wreaked havoc on the wetlands around the coastal areas and the islands off the coast of New Orleans by eating all the plant life, including the roots, and burrowing under the ground so that the land becomes weak and washes into the sea, never to return.

Imagine thousands of 20 pound rats crawling through huge labyrinths of gopher holes just under the surface.

These swamp rats, or "Coypus", which is their scientific name, are greatly accelerating coastal erosion of the wetlands, which, in turn, makes the area more vulnerable to hurricanes.

The wetlands were not long ago covered with trees, ferns, and all kinds of green fauna, are now a desolate gray wasteland with mostly dry brown grass that looks like a battlefield.

These creatures become mature enough to mate between the ages of 4 to 6 months, and each female bears one to thirteen offspring in each litter, which she will deliver twice a year and can be pregnant with a third in the same span.

Native to South America, they were brought here during the great depression of the 1930's by an entrepreneur for the fur trade. It was a very profitable enterprise for many people for a good number of years. Then, in the 70's and 80's there were movements that decried the killing of animals for fur, so the business dried up, and most of the Nutria were set free, or escaped, or were abandoned.

So the businesses, which had kept the population in check, were now no longer viable. But of course the big Swamp Rats kept reproducing until their population reached 25 million.

The State of Louisiana has tried to eradicate these varmints by putting a five dollar bounty on each tail, so there are roving bands of bounty hunters who make a decent living killing the giant gophers.

New Orleans is not the only region where these pests are found. They have been reported to be proliferating in several different European countries and in some South Asian countries such as Viet-Nam.

They have also recently been found in the Sacramento Delta.

Some experts have even theorized that these Nutria are responsible for the tilting of the Millennium Tower.

Now calm down. That was a joke.

This is not: Given their vegetarian diet, they make for a lean and clean meat, and local celebrity chefs around New Orleans have experimented with Nutria meals to try to create a market.

You may rest assured that there were a few scenes in the movie that showed people cooking and eating those big boys in various types of recipes.

There were also isolated reports of them getting into the sewer system and ending up coming up in some toilets.

There are some who think it's a crying shame to let all those pelts go to waste, they are trying to spark the fur industry all over again. In any case, they are busy designing and making coats, hats, leg warmers and the like out of these soft and beautiful rat skins.

I haven't even mentioned the protagonist in this movie, a very intriguing fisherman/philosopher who knows what life is about. Eighty year old Thomas Hernandez is the unofficial 'guide' through the bayou during the film, showing where the nutria are, and dispensing down-home philosophy as he goes.

When he isn't busy working, i.e., hunting, fishing, killing Nutria, he's busy eating, drinking and partying.

To see him dancing was a pleasure in and of itself, and then with his wife, who is quite a lovely woman in her own right. Watching the two of them together and seeing how obviously in love with each other they are is a treat in itself.

The whole Nutria situation is a very unusual phenomenon that most people, especially around these parts, are not really aware of.

This documentary may not be for everyone, but I thought it was fascinating and I wanted to share it with all of you.

Free Solo

With Alex Honnold

This is a documentary about rock climbing. No, not rock climbing, a documentary about scaling sheer granite walls thousands of feet in height.

No, not just scaling sheer granite walls thousands of feet in height, doing it without the benefit of ropes or any other traditional rock climbing safety equipment.

Thus the title, Free Solo.

Alex Honnold, who you would have to call the pre-eminent rock climber in the world, is the first and only man to complete the three thousand foot climb of the sheer granite face of El Capitan in Yosemite with nothing but his bare hands.

With just his bare hands and feet. No ropes, no safety equipment, *no nothing.*

Three thousand feet of sheer vertical granite.

Filmed by award winning National Geographic cameraman Jimmy Chin and crew, who were all experienced climbers, we get to see first hand and close up this remarkable and singular feat.

That is, when we could crawl out from under our seat in the movie theater.

Even though I knew he had done it, even though I knew he didn't die, I couldn't help myself. I had to keep reminding myself he was still alive and that he had made it to the top. But I was still on the edge of my seat. I have never squirmed so much in a movie in my life. I wanted to leave. My palms were sweating. I was holding my breath. Trying to hide. It was torture.

But I had to watch.

It was very interesting that some of the camera crew had to look away while filming.

While I was writing this review, I took another look at the previews on my computer, and got weak in the knees all over again.

This was as much a movie about rock climbing as it was a study about the man who did it, and what drives him, his lack of fear, his upbringing, and his philosophical outlook.

Very, very interesting. And *very* well done. The photography is incredible.

There was much talk about 'perfection' by Alex Honnold, because that is exactly what it takes to complete a free solo climb. It has to be perfect, because if it isn't, the result is death.

Go see this one. It will amaze you. If you can take it.

Crazy Rich Asians

Hey! We want to be cool. We want to be IN. With it. We need to know what's happening, man. So when we heard that the movie 'Crazy Rich Asians' was the Number One movie in the USA, we knew we had to go and see it.

So we went to one of these new-fangled theaters where the seats are reserved, and you can sit back in your big leather recliner and drink beer and wine while watching your movie.

Now, we didn't do any drinking, but we certainly were comfortable.

So then the lights went down, the credits came on and the movie started. And we started waiting for something to happen.

We're still waiting.

I'd like some of you who have already seen it to explain to me how this could possibly be the Number One Movie in the country.

Because *nothing happens.* There is no plot, the dialogue is vapid, and it is just about the most insipid, lifeless thing I can ever remember having the misfortune to sit through.

Seriously, it's like a soap opera without the drama.

There are a whole bunch of great looking young Asian folks going around from palace to palace in their first class accommodations, talking about nothing, and doing less.

I had one of my favorite 32-year-olds try to explain it to me and she said it's about a couple who are going to get married, and the groom's mother doesn't care for the bride-to-be.

Yes, there was that.

But is that enough to make an entire movie about? Well, you could, I guess, but this one ain't it.
You want to be put to sleep? Go see this one. But just remember this: That will be two hours of your life that you can never get back.

Rock of Ages

Starring Tom Cruise, Alec Baldwin, Russell Brand, Paul Giamatti, Catherine Zeta-Jones, Mary J. Blige and several other dweebs

There are some distinct advantages to getting on in years. For instance, for me anyway, a lot of the time I don't comb my hair. As a matter of fact, I don't even own a comb or a brush. It is kind of cool, actually, because it doesn't even matter. When we went to see this movie, I caught a glimpse of myself in the mirror, and my hair looked like I had just gotten out of bed. I started laughing to myself, because I thought of all the times when I was a teenager and everything HAD to have been perfect, or I couldn't even leave the house. Anyway, the reason I bring this up now is that this was definitely the most interesting thing that happened during this particular movie-going experience.

Oh, it started out okay. They were belting out songs even before the credits started to roll. And I remember thinking, this is kind of Oklahoma-ish, and Hey! That's OK! And it was okay. For about the first 25 or thirty songs. Which all sounded alike. But then, for the next fifty or sixty songs, I had to deliberately try to think of something else while they were singing, or I would have run out of the theater screaming. I remember thinking, it would really be nice to have a chain saw right now, because I could fire it up, and cut through the wall and see what's playing in the next theater.

Don't get me wrong. There were some funny parts in this movie. And they were absolutely worth seeing, if you are masochistic enough to sit through roughly 200 songs that all sounded exactly the same.

I will say that Tom Cruise is absolutely brilliant in his part as a crazed, doped-out-alcoholic rock star, but: Alec Baldwin singing a duet with Russell Brand? That's almost as bad as Meryl Streep making Mama Mia. No, I take that back. It's worse. It may not have been so bad, even though they tried to spice it up by having those two in a non-heterosexual relationship, but it came on at about the three and a half hour mark, so things were quite tedious by then. Are you getting the idea that this movie was a little long? Lemme put it this way: War and Peace was a walk in the park.

As Oklahoma-ish as this movie was, though, there were some great scenes, and by great I mean weird, off-the-chain scenes involving tongues, pool tables, leg-spreading and singing into someone's buttocks. If you can stand sitting through around 500 songs that all involve the same tune, then go ahead. But you might want to bring a chain saw just in case.

Shoplifters

Saw some reviews of this one a while back, looked good, and finally got around to seeing it, and I'm sure glad we did, because this is a beautiful movie. Heartfelt. Moving.

It's about a family, well, kind of a family, a sort of down and out family, just scraping by. More like an extended family, but some of them are related and some are kind of related, it's a little confusing, but that isn't important.   There's a grandmother, a dad and mom, and two young women, an adolescent boy and a four year old girl. They all live together in this run down two room… I don't know what to call it, well, I guess you'd call it an apartment. Right in the middle of some city in Japan. (It's in Japanese with English subtitles).

One evening, as the Dad and boy are coming home from a shoplifting excursion, they come across the aforementioned four year old, who has been left alone, and they take her in. I won't go any further than that regarding the plot, just know that it's about love and honor and integrity and it is really very touching.

'Emotional delicacy' was the term used in one description of this movie, and that is quite apt.

One of the best movies I've seen in quite some time.

This one will stay with you.

VICE

This one was really something. Fresh! Exciting! Brilliant, even! For about the first 15 or 20 minutes. Then, it kind of tapered off. With highlights of brilliance here and there.

It's basically a hit piece about Dick Cheney, done up as a what? Is it a comedy? A documentary? A drama? Or all three? It's kind of Micheal Moore-ish, to a degree. But funnier.

It was very well done. Christian Bale *IS* Dick Cheney. Honest to god, he looks more like Dick Cheney than Dick Cheney himself. He is just terrific playing the former vice-president.

All these people who play real life characters do a damn good job. Sam Rockwell plays George W. and except for his thin face, he's got ol' 'W' down perfectly. And Steve Carell as Donald Rumsfeld is amazing.

Amy Adams is excellent as Mrs. Dick Cheney.

Definitely worth seeing, because there are shades of brightness throughout. But it also gets tedious in between those shades.

But here's the thing: It is so perfect for those first 15 or 20 minutes that you can't possibly expect them to keep that up for the whole movie.

That's why we're not raving about it.

Bohemian Rhapsody
Starring Rami Malek

Finally got around to seeing Bohemian Rhapsody, the movie based on the rock group 'Queen.'

One of the reasons I put off seeing this film is because with the exception of their classic 'Somebody To Love', I've never really cared for any of their music.

But after Rami Malek won the best actor Oscar I figured maybe there's something to it after all.

Carol had already seen it, so while she was teaching a dance lesson, I dropped by the theater alone and took it in.

And later that night I had a horrible nightmare about an enormous gay beaver eating my house.

I am not kidding.

Now, we all know that the real Freddy Mercury had an overbite. Or as we used to call it before political correctness set in, *BUCK TEETH.*

And we know they wanted to make Malik look as much like the character he was portraying as possible.

So they did. In spades.

But seriously, did they have to make him look like the Hamster That Ate New York?

I mean, please.

It was a hideous spectacle. That boy was *really* hard to look at. No wonder I had nightmares. He could hardly close his mouth over those enormous fake dentures, and when he did, he looked like a cross between Don Knotts and Francis the Talking Mule.

No matter how hard you concentrate, this was a sight you cannot unsee.

Other than that, the movie was pretty okay. Showed his struggle with being gay, and his eventual death from aids.

The music was better than I expected. Always nicer on the big screen. I even started to like 'We Are The Champions.'

But if you go, be ready to shield your eyes.

The Wedding Guest
Starring Dev Patel

Reviewed by Screamin' Leeman

Ah, yes, the Wedding Guest. Not to be confused with the Wedding Singer, or the Wedding Planner, or the Wedding Crashers or any other of the 200 movies about weddings, all of which have got to be better than this dog.

First of all, it is NOT about a wedding. It's about a kidnapping. A kidnapping that takes place before the wedding takes place. Why they called this the Wedding Guest is beyond me, because the protagonist (Dev Patel) wasn't a wedding guest, he was a kidnapper.

I'm sure we all enjoyed Mr. Patel in 'Lion', or 'Slumdog Millionaire', but this ain't them.

This is a piece of crap.

As the movie opens we see Dev preparing for his trip from London to Pakistan, with the sole purpose of kidnapping the bride. Nothing romantic here, he's been hired to do the deed. Why? To get her out of the arranged marriage, so that she could be with her real boyfriend. But when they finally meet, there is only acrimony between them and then, in a squabble over money, Dev kills him. And no one cares.

I mean, if *she* doesn't care, then why should we?

We didn't care about Dev, his character, the bride, or her dead boyfriend. As a matter of fact, we didn't give a rat's ass about anyone. Because in order to care for a character, the storyteller needs to make them human, to create some kind of empathy. Give us a chance to feel something for them.

But when you leave that out, then what have you got?

The whole movie doesn't make much sense, there is no way anyone who sees it could muster up any concern whatsoever about any of the characters, and the way it ended was just plain stupid.

One of the reasons I wanted to see it is that it was filmed in Pakistan and around New Delhi, where I spent some time many years ago, but they somehow managed to make that boring as well.

Don't waste your time or your money.

Us

A Film by Jordan Peele

Lotta buzz out there about 'Us'. Lots of folks are real excited, can't wait to see it.

Based on the fact that Jordan Peele's 'Get Out' was such a fabulously original and brilliant film, we rushed out to see it on the day it opened.

We were disappointed, to say the least. It seemed more like some far-fetched Stephen King piece (and by Stephen King piece I mean vague, stupid, and pointless) than the work of the genius who made Get Out.

So of course I figured, *"It must be me."*

Turns out it was, but only to a certain extent.

Because the movie is about more than just a family of look-alikes (doppelgängers) terrorizing the original family. It's about the 'dark' side in Us. In all of us, in society as a whole, the evil imbedded in our culture. Us as a nation.

About the 'otherness' we fear in others, but deny in ourselves.

The whole movie is one big metaphor.

The thing is, I don't want have to read thirty-five pages of material to figure out what the movie's about. That's why I go to movies. To be *shown*.

I don't want to have to dig deep into our collective psyche to get the meaning of a movie.

Metaphors have their place. So does symbolism, which this one is full of.

So what?

One of my favorite lines from another reviewer was this:
" 'Us' is liable to frustrate people who crave plot points that can be coherently explained…"

That really says it all. A little too esoteric for me.

But I did have nightmares about nearby people screaming horrible torturous anguished pain.

Interesting.

At Eternity's Gate

With Wilhem Dafoe as Vincent Van Gogh

Okay, this one is really a doozy. You want a sure cure for insomnia? Go see At Eternity's Gate. You'll be sleeping like a baby in no time.

As some of you know, I've been belly aching for years now about how slow most Clint Eastwood movies are. How he draws out scenes, always making sure that no blade of grass goes unnoticed.

Well, let me tell you, this one makes Clint Eastwood movies look like the Keystone Cops.

This was the story of Vincent Van Gogh in his 'Blue' period.

No, I just made that up.

It was the story of Vincent Van Gogh in some period or other, but neither one of us could stay awake long enough to figure it out.

At those times when we were mercilessly pulled from our peaceful slumber, we saw a tortured Wilhem Dafoe running across a field, or walking through the woods, or laughing to himself about some imaginary thing or other.

Then, in a few minutes…. *Oh. Huh? Where was I? …* Oh, sorry, I fell asleep for a minute.

This movie is exactly one hour and fifty minutes long. The reason I'm telling that you is because if you go, you'll want to set your alarms.

Deconstructing the Beatles: Abbey Road side one

May 25, 2019

I don't know about you, but when I see the name 'Beatles' in print on a billboard, on a magazine, on a boxcar, or even better, on a marquee, I always stop to take a look.

Because I'm a Beatle lover through and through.

So when we saw that 'Deconstructing the Beatles: Abbey Road side one' was playing at the Rafael, there was no hesitation. We bought tickets and got in there.

Now, when I say Beatle lover I'm talking about their music. Oh, sure, the guys themselves are just fine, especially our dear deceased John Lennon, but please.

It's the music, folks.

I'm writing this as a warning to other Beatle lovers who would expect to hear some Beatles music in a film with their name on it. If you go to this film expecting to hear some Beatles music, you will be very disappointed, because there *isn't any.*

To be fair, there are a few, and I mean a <u>very</u> few, little teeny refrains, each one lasting about 8 seconds.

What there mainly is, is some pompous, annoying, blow-hard standing up there telling us, in minute detail, just how each and every song on side one of the Beatles album Abbey Road was put together.

Which tracks were laid down first, then what came later, and what specific machine they used to get the sound just right.

Explaining the difference, in great unexpurgated detail, between a four track sound mixer and an eight track mixer.

Now, I often joke about certain crappy movies putting us to sleep, but this time I am not kidding. This whole thing was SO boring, SO tedious, and basically SO unnecessary. It was hard to keep our eyes open.

This guy was a championship talker. And by that I mean he wouldn't shut up. He even talked over the few little refrains we were teased with. The whole time with this self-satisfied little smirk on his face *as if* he had done something.

He did something, all right. He wasted an hour and a half of everybody's time by trying to intellectualize that which does not need intellectualizing!

This was Side one of Abbey Road. And this guy went on and on for what felt like hours, flapping his jaw without cessation and basically saying very little of interest.

Can you imagine sitting through side two? God help us!

Linda Ronstadt: The Sound Of My Voice

Apparently, this movie is only playing in seven theaters across the United States. Luckily, one of them is the Christopher B. Smith Rafael Film Center in beautiful downtown San Rafael.

I say luckily, because this is one *fabulous* movie about one of the great voices of our time.

Whether on not you like Linda Ronstadt's music, this one is really worth seeing, and if you do like her, all the more reason. It's a biographical picture of her life and the great thing about it is they don't skimp on the music!

She is singing throughout the entire movie in all the different dimensions of her remarkable career. What a treat! You know, some movies about singers spend lots and lots of time talking and talking when they should have shut up and let the music play.

But not here. It shows her in her early years, and all through her long and wonderful career, belting out tunes with her amazing voice, right up until her last concert in 2009, after she discovered she had Parkinson's disease and she could no longer sing.

Her ability to do justice to all forms of music, such as Opera, jazz, and Mexican folk songs, is absolutely thrilling to watch.

We highly recommend this one.

Hustlers

With Jennifer Lopez and others

We are really embarrassed that we actually went to see this movie. You know, I like to know as little as possible about any movie beforehand, so as not to have any expectations. Usually that works. Not this time.

We realized within about 5 minutes that this was going to be the biggest piece of crap since since the invention of celluloid.

Sure, there was a bunch of T & A, but what are we? Teenage boys? They couldn't possibly put enough on the screen to make this one palatable.

JLo, who is usually a fine actress, has stooped to a new low. What, is she trying to out-do Cher, who made 'Burlesque' a few years ago? Which was bad enough in itself, but at least it had some nice dancing and singing numbers.

This one was just crap all the way through. It's about a bunch of strippers slipping mickeys into guys' drinks and running up their credit cards to astronomical amounts.

But it's so disjointed you can hardly follow the story, which is just plain stupid in the first place.

There is scene after scene of JLo strutting into a nightclub with her 'sisters' who are all decked out in the latest slutwear. Did we really need to be treated to this a dozen or more times?

And let me tell you: JLo ain't looking that hot, and some of her 'sisters' are hurting even more.

All in all, a complete waste of time.

I looked at Rotten Tomatoes just to see what they had to say and unbelievably, they're giving it a thumbs-up!

Well, who ya gonna believe?

I'm telling you, you'll be sorry.

Judy

Starring Rene Zellweger

This was a biographical sketch of Judy Garland during the last couple years of her life.

The main reason we went to see this movie was because we had seen the previews, and we were astonished at how much Rene Zellweger looked *exactly* like Judy Garland. It was really quite amazing.

So we went, and sure enough, there she was. The very image of Judy Garland as portrayed by a great actress.

She had her walk, her talk, her mannerisms, her nuances, her facial tics down pat. It was a remarkable thing to see. You've really got to appreciate someone who can depict another so perfectly.

The only problem, and something that I forgot to consider until about ten minutes into the movie, is how utterly and completely *annoying* Judy Garland was.

Her ability to be irritating was only exceeded by her capacity to be boring. And by boring, I mean tedious, bland, mind-numbing, monotonous, insipid, and dull.

Run-screaming-from-the-theater boring. Which I did. Only without the screaming.

By the way, Carol stayed, she loved it, came out with tears in her eyes.

There's no accounting for taste.

The Irishman

With Robert De Niro, Joe Pesci, and Al Pacino
Also Ray Romano and Harvey Keitel

Oh, man, did we do you all a favor! No need to thank us now, save it for later.

We sat through three and a half hours (which seemed like five) watching 'The Irishman.'

Yes, the much anticipated new movie by Martin Scorsese, which was as boring a movie as you could ever imagine.

Apparently Netflix paid for the production of this movie, so they got control of the distribution, which is why it is only going to be on the big screen for a couple weeks before being exclusively on Netflix.

So of course, the gullible public (us included) are all rushing out to see it, knowing that our window of opportunity is slim.

If they had let it go straight to Netflix they could have saved us a lot of wasted time.

Here's the deal: What if you went to a movie and *nothing happened*?

What if you went to a movie and saw the same old tired rehashed reruns from every Godfather movie ever made?

What if they took a bunch of scenes from Mean Streets, Goodfellas, The Godfather, and every other Italian gangster movie ever made and strung them all together only with a bunch of old geezers playing the lead roles?

Folks, I give you 'The Irishman.'

Martin Scorsese should be embarrassed.

Al Pacino gives a fine performance as Jimmy Hoffa, but he gets boring as well. His favorite word is the famous ten letter word that Lenny Bruce got arrested for at the Hungry i nightclub oh so many years ago. And *that* was boring.

Robert De Niro plays Frank Sheerhan (the Irishman) who was a hit man for the mob, and who allegedly whacked Jimmy Hoffa. But he seemed like he was mailing it in, and Joe Pesci… well, he played a quiet, understated, *boring* crime boss.

Ray Romano (who plays the mob lawyer), is the only one who looks relatively young and he's fricking sixty-one.

Harvey Keitel is 80, for god sakes! He has a cameo appearance is all, and I'm pretty sure he was being propped up with a 2 x 4.

I'm sorry, no one wants to see a bunch of 76-year-olds in a movie that has already been done about 700 times. Much less sit there for *three and a half hours*!

I'm telling you, we were getting bedsores.

It was supposed to take place in the fifties and sixties so there are a series of flashbacks. Trouble is, all these guys would have been in their twenties and thirties then.

Now, in the movies you can do lots of things. But there are some things you cannot do. And one of them is you cannot make an old man young. Not with make-up, not with digital enhancements, not with whatever. Sorry. It can't be done.

Not that they didn't try. DeNiro looked like his face had been ironed. So instead of looking 76, he looked 66. Pesci is the same age as DeNiro but he looks older. They couldn't do much with him. Al Pacino looked the best. He's actually 79, but he looked about 78 and a half. Just kidding, he looked about 60, but what's the point? You just can't hide the fact that all of these guys have one foot on the banana peel.

Aside from the actors all looking like they were pulled from an assisted living facility, the plot line was filled with inconsistencies too numerous to count.

As I said: Scorsese should be embarrassed.

Here's another thing: There is no character development. How can we feel empathy if they don't give us any reason to care about them? In order to pull us into any movie, you must establish empathy. Make us *like* the actors in their roles. Show us that they're human.

A couple of token baptisms ain't gettin' it, Jack.

In this movie, the only sympathetic person was the daughter of De Niro's character, who disowned him because she knew what he was up to. And she only had about three lines, so it hardly matters.

The rest of them are a bunch of thugs that you'd cross the street to avoid.

There is one scene where Robert De Niro is walking across some rocks to dispose of a gun by throwing it in the water. And I'm thinking, *"Jesus, he better be careful, the old guy is gonna take a tumble."* But here's the thing. He's supposed to be a young man. And a thirty year old walks across rocks a lot differently than a 76 year old and there's no way you can hide that.

Did I mention embarrassing? Oh, I did? Well, okay then.

A Marriage Story

With Scarlett Johansson and Adam Driver

Ah, yes, a marriage story. Which isn't really about marriage, it's about divorce.

Remember when you got a divorce? Remember when things went bad in your marriage, remember when your arguments began to escalate? Remember when they became more and more frequent and more and more heated? Remember when you said such vile things to your partner, the one that you once loved, that you couldn't believe those words had come out of your mouth?

Remember when things got so bad you dreaded coming home? Remember when you couldn't stand to be under the same roof?

Remember getting lawyers involved and spending scads of money that you didn't really have on concepts that you really didn't agree with? Remember hearing them say *"Nobody wins in these cases?"*

Remember being so depressed and lost and feeling hopeless?

Ah, yes. A Marriage Story.

If you are nostalgic for these old times, if you've got a soft spot in your heart for the absolute hell that you once went through, well then, this movie is for you.

I'm not kidding, this one was tough.

Johansson and Driver did such a good job.

It was so *damned real.* I hated it.

Man!

Suitable Movies For Your Viewing Pleasure

By Screamin' Leeman

Thinking of going to the movies? Well, here is a handy guide of movies to see and not to see. In no particular order. You're welcome.

1. Joker

Extraordinary, remarkable performance by Joaquin Pheonix. To say this is a 'dark' movie would be an understatement. Very well done. If he doesn't win *all* of the best actor awards, no one is paying attention.

2. A Beautiful Day In The Neighborhood

There was a documentary about the life of Fred Rogers which was excellent, as is this drama with Tom Hanks. Anything with or about Mr. Rogers is wonderful. Those of us who never got those simple life affirming pieces of advice just saying *'You're okay just the way you are'* always get teary-eyed immediately.   There are other pieces about Mr. Rogers; all of them are worthwhile.

3. Once Upon A Time In Hollywood

Another very long Quentin Tarantino movie with great attention to detail that starts out slow but picks up the pace in the second half and rewards us for our patience.

4. Ford v Ferrari

If your idea of entertainment is watching Christian Bale, with a stoical look upon his face, driving in circles around a race track, seemingly endlessly, well this one's for you. Personally, I'd rather watch paint dry.

5. Jumanji: The Next Level

Someone please kill me now. We made the mistake of seeing this because a few misguided relatives, who will soon be disowned, said it was kind of good. NOT. A complete waste of time.

6. **The Irishman**

Hopefully you read my previous review so I have already saved you from wasting 3 1/2 hours of your precious time. If not, I'll be happy to pass it along.

7. **Marriage Story**

Excellent acting, excellent script. This one was tough to watch. Very real. Should be titled 'Divorce Story' because that's what it's about. *Too* real.

8. **Knives Out**

This one started out great. It was fun and fresh until about halfway through. Then it became tiresome, repetitive and boring.

9. **Rocketman**

If you're an Elton John fan I highly recommend this one. This guys voice is not in the same category as Elton's, but it's great fun just the same. Lots of songs.

10. **Linda Ronstadt: The Sound Of My Voice**

This is the best music documentary I've seen in a long, long time. I didn't realize how versatile she was. It is chock full of music and singing. Also with Dolly Parton and Emmylou Harris. Fabulous! Don't miss it!

11. **Bombshell**

About women being sexually harassed in their workplace, in particular the story of serial predator Roger Ailes, the chairman and CEO of Fox News, being brought down by three courageous women. Very well done. Tense. Excellent.

12. **Richard Jewell**

Since most Clint Eastwood movies are about 5 hours too long, I hesitate to subject myself to this one, although I heard it was good. Have you seen it?

13. **Parasite**

Omg, this is an amazing, original, fresh, funny movie that gradually evolves into a very dark film. Very interesting.

14. **Motherless Brooklyn**

Edward Norton wrote, produced, directed and starred in this movie about a detective with Tourette's Syndrome. Too bad, because what he ended up with was not only an insipid piece of crap, but an insult to those who are really afflicted with Tourette's.

15. **Hustlers**

This was a little known movie about a group of sluts who steal money from men after drugging their drinks. It stars Jennifer Lopez who should be really, really embarrassed, mortified even, as should everyone else who had anything to do with the making of this piece of trash.

16. **Uncut Gems**

Starring Adam Sandler in a non-comic role as a frenetic New York jewelry dealer who is also a compulsive gambler. Except for some glaring errors in the plot, this one is interesting, yet *frantic* from start to finish.

17. **Jojo Rabbit**

Can a movie about Adolf Hitler and Nazi Germany be funny? The jury is still out.

18. **The Good Liar**

Helen Mirren and Ian McKellen in a con-man movie that should have been a one hour TV show instead of a damn two and a half hour movie. Sheesh, you invest all that time in a movie to end up with a big fat *"So what?"*

19. **Where's My Roy Cohn?**

A straight forward look at one of the most unscrupulous, manipulative, downright evil people you could ever imagine. A former mentor of our current president, offers insights into some of his moves. Amazingly scary.

20. **David Crosby: Remember My Name**

Documentary about David Crosby from Crosby Stills Nash & Young. Surprisingly, this movie only provides proof that Mr. Crosby is a self-centered, insufferable jerk.

21. **Little Women**

Come on. Did you really think I'd go see this one?

That's all, folks!

DOWNHILL

Julia Louis-Dreyfus
Will Ferreli

Hey, ya wanna have some fun at the movies? Then go see 'Downhill.' We sure did.
Had fun, that is.

This is a remake of a 2014 Swedish movie by the name of Force Majeure, which we
had never heard of, thank you.

I suppose it's billed as a comedy, and there are a lot of laughs, but it is also a drama
about a guy who panics and ditches his family as an avalanche heads toward them.

I'm not giving anything away here, this is what the movie is about. So although it has
some laughs, there is also a serious side. Some are calling it a 'different kind' of a
disaster movie.

Of course, it brings up the question for anyone who is watching: What would I do? All of
us like to think we'd be heroes and protect our family. But when that moment of panic
comes, when all of a sudden you're in a life or death situation, well, what would you do?

Julia Louise-Dreyfus is excellent as the over-bearing control-freak mother, and Will
Ferrell is just as good as the passive dad.

In any case, it is done very well. Very real. And, there are a lot of laughs, and some
very serious moments, and some very touching moments, and a few characters, all of
whom are exceptional, each in their own special way.

I loved it!

The Cabin In The Woods

A long time ago, I heard a very old person talking about the things they missed most, and one of the things mentioned was "there's no more surprises." I remember thinking wow, that's interesting... And as I myself creep up in years, I understand, to an extent, just what they meant by that. For instance: When my darling children, who are in their twenties, tell me about this great movie they've seen and then I go see it, and realize I've seen movies like this a hundred times before... Still, it is a great movie for them, because they are young and it is exciting and fresh and new, but for me, it's just another helping of the same old stuff!

I've seen it before, and I've seen most of 'em. No more surprises.

So you need to show me something new, something fresh. It has ALL been done before, but show me a different take, something that I can get excited about.

Which brings me to our movie, The Cabin In The Woods. You've heard of it of course, it's a horror/slasher/sci-fi/zombie flick.

Yes, it is fresh. Yes, it is new. Yes, it is exciting.

Let me just say this: About half way through, when I couldn't make head nor tail of what seemed like an absurd plot, I figured, okay, probably they won't ever tie this thing together, but hopefully it won't matter as long as they bring on the mayhem.

But, tie it together they did, very, very neatly. And the mayhem? When the s--t starts to hit the f-n, you'll sit up in your seat and your eyes will widen. This is Mayhem with a capital M.

This isn't for everyone, that's for sure. And I certainly am not going to spoil it for you by outlining the plot. But I will say that there are a couple movies that were supposed to be violent, bloody. For instance, Quentin Tarantino's 'From Dusk Till Dawn' comes to mind, and then there was this movie from new Zealand about some misdeeds with a lawnmower, supposed to be the bloodiest movie of all time. And I was thinking, in the middle of "Cabin," that Dusk to Dawn might as well have been Mr. Hulots Holiday and the so-called bloodiest movie of all time... it's got NOTHING on this flick.

I'm telling you, this one made me high. I was laughing when I left the theater. I was giddy, just as when I left 'Inglorious Basterds.' Why? Because something different happened, that's why. Same as the first 'Alien.' I was high from that one because they didn't follow the same pattern of all movies since the beginning of time.

And here, finally, is another movie that dares to veer off the beaten path. I highly recommend it to... Well, you know who you are.

Tiny Tim: King For A Day
Documentary About The Life And Times Of Tiny Tim

Went to the movies in an actual theater this past weekend. First time in over a year. It really hardly mattered what the movie was, I was just very happy to be able to drag myself and the little woman to a safe place where we could watch a movie on the big screen.

Carol had been very concerned about entering some godforsaken hell hole that was reeking with covid, but I told her that the theater was fumigated between movie times with Clorox, and if we went to the first showing we'd have a pretty good chance of coming out alive.

It was playing at the Rafael theater in beautiful downtown San Rafael, and as some of you saw on Facebook, we had the entire theater to ourselves.   Well, for a few minutes, anyway. Then three others showed up, so there was a quintet of us watching.

What a pleasure to sit back in a darkened auditorium and watch a movie. We took this all for granted until the pandemic changed everything around. But ever so slowly now, things may be getting back to normal.

Some of you folks may not be old enough to remember the Tiny Tim phenomenon. So ask your parents. But some of us are. He was a real weirdo, and he played it up. I had his album. No matter what else anyone could say about the man, whether true or not, the one thing I know is he could sing like a bird. He had a beautiful voice, although there wasn't quite enough of it in this movie.

But it was very interesting anyway, I didn't realize (or I had forgotten) how big he really got in 1968-69. Of course there were quite a lot of other things going at that time, so forgive me if I didn't notice.

I mean, for god sakes we had the peace marches ramping up big time, we were trying to end the Vietnam War. There was the trial of the Chicago Seven, the assassination of Martin Luther King that sparked riots across the country. Robert Kennedy was assassinated. Richard Nixon got elected President. There were violent protests among us anti-war demonstrators and police. Muhammed Ali was serving a suspension from boxing while waiting for the U. S. Supreme Court to rule on his conviction of being a conscientious objector. AND that was the year I got kicked out of the Boy Scouts.

And then there was Tiny Tim. He made the covers of every magazine in the country (which was one of the ways fame was measured in those days). He was all over the front pages of all the gossip rags.

His most famous song was "Tiptoe Through The Tulips" sung in his famous high falsetto voice accompanied by himself playing his ukulele. And I'll tell you, the man could flat out sing.

He sang about love and yearning. I don't remember the name of the song, but I remember some of the lyrics:

"All I want is fifty million dollars,
And if Tuesday Weld would only be my wife,
If I only owned the Pennyvania Railroad,
Then I would be satisfied for life…"

One of the biggest things he ever did was actually get married to a young woman called 'Miss Vicki' live on the Johnny Carson show. That show had the second biggest audience in the history of television. Only the first moon landing was bigger.

He had a heart attack on stage and died during a performance in 1996 at the age of 64.

A fascinating documentary about a strange guy and some turbulent times.

Trial Of The Chicago 7

With Yahya Abdul-Mateen II, Sacha Baron Cohen, Michael Keaton, Joseph Gordon-Levitt, Frank Langella, Eddie Redmayne, Mark Rylance, Jeremy Strong, and Ben Shenkman.

Want to get all riled up again at the blatant injustice and non-objectivity of Judge Julius Hoffman, just as many of us were in 1969? Then take a look at 'The Trial Of The Chicago Seven' on Netflix. Oh, man, about three-quarters of the way through, I had to pause it... I was shaking, my stomach was turning over, I needed a break.

I was feeling the same anger and frustration that many of us felt in 1969, as Julius Hoffman presided over the charade that has become known as the Trial Of The Chicago Seven.

"This is my courtroom, I'll rule as I see fit." --Judge Julius Hoffman.

"I'm not used to being tried for my thoughts." --Abbie Hoffman.

For those of us who were around then, you'll be able to relive your exasperation and disgust at the misguided, contemptuous, and downright illegal way that Julius Hoffman conducted this trial.

He not only made a travesty of justice, but was openly contemptuous of the defendants. At one point he bound and gagged Black Panther Bobby Seale for protesting not having legal representation. The entire trial was a miscarriage of justice, and a circus performance by Abbie Hoffman and Jerry Rubin.

This was the first time that the defendants chose not to follow ordinary court procedures and rules. This was a political trial, a point that Abbie Hoffman made throughout the film. It was the Establishment against the protesters.

In this case, the Establishment was Mayor John Daly of Chicago and the riots that were created by his own police state.

So much went down during that trial that didn't make it into the movie, but still: It is a riveting film from start to finish.

Highly recommended.

Nomadland

With Frances McDormand

Finally got around to seeing this year's Oscar Winner for Best Picture. My first thought was: Wow. This must have been a real slow year.

That's what we had heard. 'It's kind of slow…' Or words to that effect.

One friend, who really liked it a lot, said "It kind of drags."

All these are understatements.

Here's an example: Carol and I watched it at home. At one point it paused all by itself, but it took us several minutes to realize that it wasn't part of the movie.

We had to check with each other: "Did it stop?"

It's also very dark.

As in we couldn't see what was on the screen.

Remember that movie with Bruce Darn of a few years ago? "Nebraska?" About an old guy in a cold, bleak landscape?

Well, compared to this one, that looked like the Music Man.

And another thing: Hey Frances, we know you're above it all, but could you have cleaned yourself up a bit before accepting the Award? Maybe combed your hair?

In The Heights

Look, the first thing you have to know is that if you go to see this movie, it's probably a good idea to take a sleeping bag.

Because you're going to be in there for a long, long, time.

Oh, the movie was pretty good, it was based on the New York play about a certain neighborhood in NY City; Washington Heights, which is mostly full of people from the Dominican Republic who love to sing and dance and wear bright colors.

And man, it was loaded with lots of great music, and some (not enough, in my opinion) great dance numbers as well.

But, dammit, it was WAY too long.

My boy Jesse went with us, and he took two naps and finished the book he was reading.

You know the old saying "Leave 'em wanting more"? The folks who made this one obviously had never heard that.

Listen, after you've been in there for over two hours, you start to get fidgety. And at two and a half hours…. Oh, man, they were really testing our limits.

They could have cut an HOUR out of this, and they still would've had a fine movie, and we'd probably have left the theater actually wanting more.   But we were in there so long we were getting bedsores. So you start thinking weird thoughts. Such as how can I get out of here without being seen? Is this damn thing EVER going to end? And this is getting monotonous… What *was* a great time and a lot of fun has now become a chore…. And that's no good.

The Adjustment Bureau

With Matt Damon and Emily Blunt

We rushed right out to see this one, and let me tell you, it was unbelievable! And I mean that in the truest sense of the word. No, *literally.* I mean it was implausible, improbable, inconceivable, and impossible, not to mention just plain stupid.

What I want to know is: What were we thinking? What happened? I mean, how many times do I have to go to a Matt Damon film before it sinks in? Didn't we walk out of 'Inception' just a couple of months ago?   How could I have forgotten so soon?

Guess I'll chalk it up to getting fooled by the previews...

The premise of the story was that there are a bunch of "Guys With Hats On" who control everything we do. They only show up when something goes wrong, or when something doesn't go according to "The Plan." And the premise of *this,* or at least the explanation that is given by one of the top "Guys With a Hat," is that we really screwed up the world, so they had to step in with some kind of "Master Plan" so that everything will work out just fine. Yeah. That makes sense. *Say, your "Master Plan" is really working well now, isn't it?*   Who the hell writes this stuff?

Anyway, Matt Damon meets this woman (Emily Blunt) in a men's restroom (how quaint) then the "Guys Who Are Wearing Hats" decide that this wasn't part of the plan, so the rest of the movie is spent trying to separate them, and them finding ways to get back together. And let me tell you, just rehashing it now makes me want to puke. This thing is so lame, so thoughtless, and so just plain dumb that I am shaking my head in amazement.   It was agonizing, sitting through that piece of crap, hoping beyond hope that they'd pull it together somehow at the end. Yeah. Sure. *NOT!*

Spending a couple hours getting splinters would have been more fun.

Carol has joyfully accepted her instructions: That if I ever even suggest, ever, seeing anything with Matt Damon in it, she is to take off her shoe, and if she isn't wearing spike heels, to change into them, then take one of them off, clutch it with both hands held high above her head, and bring it down with full force upon my forehead.

Maybe I need to put it in print so that I can use it as a reference. Remember in the movie 'Memento?' Where the guy was going in and out of an amnesia state, and so he tattooed things on his arms that he needed to remember?   If you see me one of these days with a tattoo on my arm that says *"NEVER, EVER GO TO A MATT DAMON MOVIE, EVER,"* I'm sure you'll understand.

Don't Look Up

With Meryl Streep, Jennifer Lawrence, Leonardo DiCaprio, Jonah Hill, Kate Blanchett, Tyler Perry, Ariana Grande, and others
Reviewed by Screamin' Leeman

This is a hilarious satire on the state of our culture, and the misinformation that is spewed at us daily from all sides.

Although it is a parody, it certainly rings true. The preview says 'Based On Real Events… That Haven't Happened.' Which pretty well sums it up.

The premise is that two scientists, while tracking the trajectory of a huge comet, realize that it is heading directly toward earth
and when it hits it will destroy our planet and all life forms on it.

So obviously, they need to tell the world.

But because of the short attention span of the general public, and all the misinformation, fake news, etc. out there, getting the word out becomes a little more difficult than you might think.

Meryl Steep does a perfect parody of a certain former orange tinted president. And Jonah Hill, as her son and Chief of Staff, is brilliant as a non-caring, self-centered bastard. Kate Blanchett does a fabulous job as Kelly Ripa while Tyler Perry, as her sidekick, fills in the Michael Strahan part beautifully.

There are so many little hilarious (and infuriating) pieces to this movie. It *really* rings true.

The cool thing is, is that it's on Netflix, so you can watch it anytime in the comfort of your own pig sty. Oops, I meant the comfort of your own home.
Highly recommended.

West Side Story
A Steven Spielberg Production

You know, I've heard that some people criticized this remake because they said the guy who plays Tony is not right. Or that he doesn't have a powerful voice. Or whatever. And there are other criticisms as well.

I guess you can find something wrong with anything.

But this is West Side Story! As done by Steven Spielberg. What could be wrong?

Answer: Absolutely nothing! This is a brilliant remake of a timeless story by *The Master.*

The cinematography is brilliant, as is the lighting, and the dancing and singing are breathtaking.

It is a classic story full of singers with beautiful voices, and wonderful dance routines.

I don't know if it is streaming yet, but this is definitely one you should see on the big screen.

And by the way, 'Tony' has a beautiful voice.

A fabulous, touching, delightful movie experience.

I can't wait to see it again!

House Of Gucci

With Lady Gaga, Adam Driver, Salma Hayack, Al Pacino

It's funny how two people can go to a movie and come out with wildly different impressions.

Carol loved this one. She loved how the story unfolded, she loved the acting, the pace, the sets, the development.

She told me she loved everything about this movie.

I, on the other hand, can't remember when I've had the misfortune to have to sit through this kind of drivel. I was so sorry I didn't have any weapons on me, so I could have put myself out of my misery. I was looking around on the floor for a discarded plastic bag to put over my head, but no such luck.

Which meant I had to sit through what felt like 6 hours of guys wearing their overcoats draped over their shoulders, women wearing giant sunglasses, and everyone smoking like a chimney. I swear, Gaga must have gone through a couple of cartons of smokes. She was lighting up in every frame. I got a cough just from watching.

Not only that, but all of the actors, both men and women, were speaking in ridiculous, overblown Italian accents that made them hard to understand. So I missed about 75 percent of the dialogue. But that didn't matter that much because NO ONE CARES.

When even Al Pacino sounds phony doing an Italian accent, you know there's a problem.

I was actually toying with the idea of seeing Scream 12, or 16, or 28, whatever number they're up to now, which was playing next door, but in the end opted to see the Gucci pic.

BIG mistake.

Seeing a few teenagers get slashed at least would have kept me awake.

Nobody

With Bob Odenkirk, Connie Nielsen, FZA, Christopher Lloyd

There are bad movies, there are good movies. There are movies where your mind wanders, and movies that keep you focused. And then there are movies that lock you in, with exactly the right amount of superfluous stuff, and keep you on the edge of your seat for the entire movie.

This is one of those.

A terrific revenge movie.

You know, mild mannered family man who used to be some kind of an operative. Trying to live a nice quiet life, but deep inside, yearning to wreak havoc and hurt people.

And the great thing about this one is that the bad guys are defined very well, so we're all really, really happy to see them maimed, or killed, or both.

It is _very_ well done. Nothing wasted here (except the dirt bags).

Remember those old Charles Bronson movies in the seventies? The Death Wish series? Great revenge films, only old Chuck didn't really take it far enough, in my opinion. There was way too much in-between stuff. Too much fluff. And not nearly enough revenge.

Then along came 'A History Of Violence', which really set the pace. That one was quite satisfying.

And now, here is 'Nobody', which turns it up a couple notches from there. You wanna see a bunch of scum balls get their brains beat out and killed? This is the one for you.

The mayhem gets really crazy as it goes on, but it's all in good fun.

Now, Chuck Bronson just killed a few select dirt balls. And Viggo Morteneson, in History Of Violence, killed a few more guys who all deserved it, but in this one the job gets finished. He kills ALL of them.

Check it out. (We saw it on HBO).

The Shape Of Water

Starring Sally Hawkins

This is the heartwarming story of a young woman and an aardvark. No, wait. Sorry.

A girl and a lizard. Oops, *just kidding.*

Really, it's the enchanting tale of the Creature From The Black Lagoon meets Snow White and they go dancing with Busby Berkeley.

A lovely film (for some).

No, seriously, this one is an other-worldly fairy tale about hooking up with animals. No, wait. That is far too simple.

It's not about bestiality.

There have been lots of movies about relationships between humans and animals. King Kong comes to mind. Also, Joe Joe the Dog Faced Boy Meets the Platypus.

And let us not forget the great kung-fu film of a few years back: Hidden Hamster, Flying Goat.

No, this one is a love story. A tender, touching, fantasy that is *not* about animal husbandry.

It's about relationships with non-humans. Or, I should say about a relationship between a human and a large codfish.

Well, not exactly a fish, more like a half man, half reptile that likes to go swimming.

Now, remember Francis the Talking Mule?

Well, he isn't in it.

Neither is Mr. Ed.

But seriously, this is a fantasy tale where the characters are defined in comic book terms. In other words, you definitely know who the bad guys are. And who the sweet innocent young things are.

Guys, take your wives or girlfriends. Or both. Show 'em your soft side.

You need to suspend your belief in reality, and go with your imagination.

If you can do that, I'm sure you'll be able to stay awake.

Wait a minute. I'm kidding around here, but many people think this is a pretty good movie. Lots of folks, including my wife, adored it. It is nominated for lots of awards, including Best Picture.

It ain't no Forrest Gump (thank god), but it also is not the Texas Chainsaw Massacre.

It is so easy to have a few laughs at director Guillermo del Toro's expense.

But really, I think I kind of liked it. Maybe.

Sort of.

Snore.

'Get Out' was *WAY* better.

San Andreas

Starring Arnold Schwartzenager, oh wait, no, It was Dwayne 'The Rock' Johnson

Yep, it's a new generation.

Now, instead of a body builder turned actor, we have an ex-Wrestle Mania Star turned big screen idol. Yes, ladies and gentlemen, I give you.... *Dwayne Johnson!*

In case you didn't know, this movie is about the biggest earthquake to ever roll through California, and roll through California it does.

Phew.

After reducing Los Angeles to a huge pile of smoking rubble, it moves right up to San Francisco, where it commences to do the same.

Man! Just like a wrestling match, the action is fast and furious! They don't waste any time at all. First thing is a daring helicopter rescue by our hero of a young blond woman (what else) hanging off a cliff in her wrecked SUV. Very precarious, some serious hitches along the way, but of course our hero prevails just as the SUV plummets into the canyon.

Shortly after that, earthquakes start slamming the entire state of California.

I'm telling you, folks, there is very little down time in this movie. Oh, there is one scene where Arnold, I mean Dwayne, and his ex-wife are talking about the child they lost... Her name was Mallory, or Valerie, or Hillary, or Celery... In any case, the three minutes talking about her was just about the only three minutes in the entire movie that wasn't jam packed with action sequences involving every type of vehicle known to man. Helicopters, planes, boats, cars and trucks, they all get their share. As a matter of fact there is even a loaded container ship crashing into the Golden Gate Bridge from atop a tidal wave.

Oh, sorry. Did I spoil it for you?

Darn.

I went with my girls once again. My charming yet lovely wife Carol, plus Michele, Karena, and Nora, The best part of this particular movie-going-experience was looking down the row of seats every time some crazy action sequence would occur and our boy had cheated death once again, and seeing Nora, with a really silly smile on her face, giving a big thumbs up.

Glen Campbell, I'll Be Me

This movie is only playing in a few select theaters, and even then at odd times. I highly recommend making the effort to see it, because it is really something special.

It is a documentary about Glen Campbell in his waning years, as Alzheimer's disease begins to take him.

A fascinating and very touching story as we watch him try to remember what day it is, or what year, or any basic questions, but even through all the memory loss, he somehow retains his ability to play the guitar and sing and perform on stage.

And let me tell you, that boy knows his way around a git-fiddle. He can flat out *play!* That shouldn't really be surprising, because he started his career as a studio musician, and he has cut records with the best of them.

The movie is a chronicle of his last tour, after he was diagnosed with Alzheimer's. They play over a hundred dates in venues all across America, and we get a behind the scenes look at what he is like, and from all I've seen, he seems like a genuine nice guy. Happy, easy, playful.

Early on, as the tour is starting, there is tension, because no one really knows if he is going to be okay or not. But his stage presence is really something. He is so relaxed. And he does just fine, mostly.

The movie is narrated by his current wife, who I didn't know anything about, but it is obvious how much she cares for him, and vice versa. She's quite a bit younger than him (he turns 77 during the filming) and they have some kids together who seem to be in their twenties.

Three of his kids are on the tour, playing in the band. It is so nice to see the relationship he has with his daughter as they do some really fabulous duets together, him on guitar and her playing banjo, even though at times he struggles to remember her name.

The folks that made this movie wanted to show what it was like to deal with Alzheimer's, and they did a terrific job. It is genuinely touching, maybe more so, because, even though we may not all have been huge Glen Campbell fans, we are familiar with him, and who he is, so it is like we know him. He's like a friend.

They show some trips to the doctors office as the story rolls along and it is interesting and sad to see how the disease is progressing. And through it all Glen is, for the most part, cheerful, upbeat and lighthearted.

Then they cut back to the music and we are all uplifted again.

This is a very touching movie, folks. Take some kleenex.

Licorice Pizza, Scream, Jackass

In our quest to see all the Oscar-nominated films, Carol and I went to see 'Licorice Pizza' the other night. It stars a young man named Cooper Hoffman, who just happens to be the son of Philip Seymour Hoffman, and is quite an actor in his own right. This is the kind of film where, while you are waiting for something to happen, an absolutely lovely and delightful movie unfolds right before your very eyes.

It seems like a simple little movie, and it is, but there are a lot of things that happen that stick in your mind and you find yourself thinking about long after it's over.

I hate to label it good, clean, wholesome fun, because that may dissuade most of my friends and relatives, but please, just disregard that and go see it anyway.

You won't be sorry.

In other movie-going news, I personally made the mistake of going to see the latest installment of **'Scream.'**

Why?

Like the story told in the "Magnificent Seven' about the guy who took off all his clothes and jumped into a cactus patch: "It seemed like a good idea at the time."

But, as I sat *alone* in the theater, I realized within about 5 minutes that this was a big mistake. So even before any of the stabbing began, I high-tailed it and went to the next theater where the **Jackass** movie was playing (thank god for six-movie complexes).

One of the interesting things about going to the movies these days is that there is hardly anyone else in the theater. Especially for crappy movies like these two.

Now, in describing Jackass, there is only one word that is fitting, and that is *embarrassing*.

There was only one other guy in the theater and I only caught a glance of him as I went and sat as far away from him as I could. He looked even older than me, and I think he had a white cane.

Still, I was embarrassed.

Could you think of anything worse than a bunch of middle aged men standing around laughing at some lame high-school prank they've just done? That was the worst.

I was embarrassed for them, I was embarrassed for the cameraman who had to shoot this group of hyenas.

I stayed because I was hoping to see something funny, and I did, actually.

There was one stunt that was like a Mack Sennett scene where they were in a furniture store and one of them was lying on this huge kind of a beanbag something and this big fat guy jumped from the top of a ladder onto the other side of the bag whereupon the other guy flew up in the air and crashed right through the ceiling. It was one of those 'hung' ceilings that you often find in furniture or other big stores, so when he went flying up he went right through the ceiling and then back through it again on the way down. It was really funny.

But please don't go see it because of this. You can watch plenty of stunts from old Mack Sennett movies, or Charlie Chaplin films or any number of things on You-Tube that are as good or better.

The problem is, is that after every stunt, they'd pan to all the guys standing around laughing.

O. M. G. !!!

Did I say embarrassing?

When the credits started to roll, I scurried out of there as fast as I could so as not to have to face the other patron in the theater, even though I'm pretty sure he was blind.

Thank god no one goes to the movies anymore. I would have been totally mortified it _anyone_ had seen me come out of there, let alone someone I actually knew.

The good thing about this whole movie-going-experience was that after my escape from **Jackass**, I went back to **Scream** and caught the final scene where the bad guy gets his due and I've got to tell you, it was really worth it.

Because they really _did it right._

You know how when the bad guys get theirs in lots of movies, and depending on just how bad they've been, we are often dissatisfied? As in, they die too quickly, or they don't suffer enough, or we don't get to see them really hurt?

Well, no worries here. This one is _very_ satisfying. It is SO over-the-top, it becomes a parody. Maybe the whole movie is a parody, I don't know. So then the final scene was a parody of a parody. In any case, I'm still laughing.

So all in all, it was worth it.

And after all that, I found out that neither of these two films are on the Oscar list.

Can you beat that?

OSCAR CONTENDERS FOR BEST MOVIE 2022: THE RUNDOWN

In no particular order

1. **CODA**

This one is about a family who has CHS really bad. The reason they all have CHS (Can't Hear Sh-t) is because they are deaf. Well, three of them anyway. The mom, the pop and the brother. The sister can hear quite clearly and she wants to be a singer. The family earns their keep by doing commercial fishing. Well, they get busted for fishing while deaf, and that creates a bunch of problems for all of them, which of course are all solved through music. Kind of like when the Hills Were Alive...

A very nice movie. Oscar material? Cute, nice, touching, but clearly not Oscar material.

2. **DON'T LOOK UP**

This one won't win the Oscar, but it's definitely my favorite. It is a hilarious satire on contemporary American life.

The movie portrays an all-too-real depiction of what happens when a couple of astronomers discover a huge planet-killing comet heading straight for Earth and what happens when they try to tell people about it.

Meryl Streep as the President (loosely based on a recent orange haired office holder) is just about perfect as is Jonah hill, who plays her son and her Chief Of Staff. With Jennifer Lawrence, Leonardo De Caprio, Cate Blanchett, Tyler Perry, Rob Morgan, and Mark Rylance. All of these people do a fabulous job. This is a terrific movie.

3. **NIGHTMARE ALLEY**

The biggest nightmare of all was trying to sit through this piece of crap where Bradley Cooper was standing around in just about every scene looking like he had just been lobotomized. Not only that but he was smoking a cigarette 100% of the time. And I mean every shot. I wonder how much the tobacco council pays to get these actors to smoke in movies? Must be substantial.

In any case, this one really drags. After about two hours went by, and nothing had developed, and nothing happened, I gave up.

You know, this was a remake of the 1947 movie of the same name which was hard enough to get through. But at least the 1947 version had a few Art Deco buildings and a couple of old cars.

4. **BELFAST**

Thank god for streaming (and subtitles). If we had seen this in a movie theater, there is no way we would have understood a single word. Everyone in the entire movie talked with a really heavy Irish accent. They might as well have been speaking Mandarin. Since I have a case of CHS too, we get subtitles with our streaming. And the subtitles saved the day. This one is a semi-autobiographical story of the youth of Kenneth Branagh. Quite real, it depicts the problems of the Catholic/Protestant warfare in the sixties. It is being touted to win the best film. But… sorry, I'm just thinking that in order to win best film, you should be able to understand the dialogue. Is that too much to ask?

5. **KING RICHARD**

You know, every time we're looking for a movie to go see, we run across this one, and we usually say "Oh, let's go see King Richard." And then after a few minutes we both realize that we've already seen it. Carol said she loved it, and I completely forgot it. Now, if you see a movie, and can't remember if you've seen it, does that mean it's you? Or is it quite a forgettable movie? I prefer to think it's the latter. Unless I forgot to take my meds, which is entirely possible.

6. **DUNE**

Could this one be as boring and tedious as the first one? Probably. If anyone sees it, let me know.

7. **LICORICE PIZZA**

Another very nice movie about young love. It stars Cooper Hoffman who is the son of Philip Seymour Hoffman and is a very good actor in his own right. Also starring Alana Haim, and her two sisters and her mom and pop. Come to find out, the rock group Haim is comprised of the three Haim sisters. How do you like that? In any case, this is a very sweet movie, quite likable. Not Oscar for Best Picture likable, but worth seeing. Once.

8. WEST SIDE STORY

This is a fabulous re-make of the original by Steven Spielberg. This is Spielberg at his best. Beautiful cinematography, fabulous singing and dancing, full of beautiful people. Absolutely wonderful.

9. DRIVE MY CAR

Oh, man, this one is really complex, and esoteric, and hard to understand and understated yet confusing and there is a story within a story and the people are all very stoic. Not only that, it is a Japanese film with subtitles but there are different subtitles (different fonts) for the different kinds of languages that are being spoken such as Indonesian, Korean, and some sign language.

A good part of the movie is taken up rehearsing 'Uncle Vanya' which is a Chekhov play which is meant to challenge the audience and/or the reader and so is this movie.

So, the protagonists were grief stricken because of loss, and they were stoic.

But here's the thing: Homie don't like stoic. Homie is not a fan of having to figure things out. Homie goes to the movies to be entertained, not to be challenged. Homie likes to see someone hit in the head with a 2 X 4 because then we know exactly what is happening.

Hey! I got yer Chekhov right here!

10. THE POWER OF THE DOG

This is a very good movie, very real. With Benedict Cumberbatch and Kirsten Dunst. Story takes place in Montana, 1925. About life on a cattle ranch. There's a hell of a lot going on in this movie. About people and relationships. It's really good. I'm thinking it should win.

ELVIS

"Well you can knock me down — step in my face,
Slander my name all over the place —
Do anything that you want to do
But uh-uh honey lay off o' my shoes"

Are you one of those people whom the next lines of this song automatically pop into your head?

Well, you need to go out and see ELVIS, the movie, right away.

The music itself is worth the trip. The cinematography is superb. They do sort of a montage of his early work and some of his later songs, and it really works well.

Look, there have been so many Elvis impersonators over the years, some good, some not so good, but the problem is, is that no one *really* looks like Elvis.

Neither does this guy, at first. But at about five minutes in, you'll forget there's a difference.

Tom Hanks is quite despicable as the evil Tom Parker which is another reason to go. He's all dressed up in a fat suit, with a huge double chin, and he is sleazingly amazing.

Now, it's about a half hour too long, and it starts to drag about two thirds of the way through, but it's saved by the music.

And that boy has the moves...

Go see it.

Barbarian

With Georgina Campbell and Bill Skarsgard and some others you've never heard of, not that it matters.

I went to see this one alone, because Carol wouldn't dream of seeing anything that's labeled 'horror.' Her loss.

She has different tastes than I; you might say more discerning. Sometimes I go to see these silly comedies, once in a while a slasher film, and about 90% percent of the time I'm disappointed. So I was prepared for another let-down, because that's the usual outcome.

But it was not a let-down at all. This was truly a work of art, and an incredibly satisfying film.

It is <u>very</u> well done.

The premise is that a woman rents an Air BnB and there's some kind of a mix up with the booking company because someone else is staying there already. But it's raining hard and the town is over booked and... she ends up staying... and... of course, things happen.

It's very real, very believable.

I can't say more, of course, because I don't want to ruin it for you.

But I will say this isn't just any old run-of-the-mill slasher film, this is a few notches above.

As a matter of fact, I realized as I was writing this, I was mesmerized.

When I left the theater, it took me quite a few minutes to get back to reality.

Highly recommended.

Triangle Of Sadness

With Woody Harrelson and others

First, let's talk about the new and improved Tiburon Movie Theater, now called the Cinelounge. You know, the Tiburon theater has been there a very long time, but recently, it has come under new ownership and it has changed for the better.

As a matter of fact, we had quite a unique movie going experience out there the other evening.

We had gone to see 'Triangle Of Sadness' on a Monday night (more about that later), and then, because we liked that particular theater so much, we decided to go back on Thursday and see 'All Guys Are Losers.'

So we drove out to Tiburon, parked in the lovely and spacious parking lot adjacent to the theater and went in, where we were greeted warmly by a member of the staff, maybe it was the owner, but in any case, he was quite friendly and accommodating (as were all the employees) as he explained to us that that particular movie was not playing on this particular evening.

As a matter of fact, when he greeted us, he asked if we were here to see a movie, which I thought was kind of strange, as we were in a movie theater. But as we were talking about the movie not being shown, he asked us if we'd like to buy a drink (they sell beer, wine, and gin and tonics, among all else) and come over to the 'Cine Room' where there was a Trivia Game going on.

So we went in to take a look, and there were a bunch of people in comfortable chairs and couches with drinks and things and there was indeed, a Trivia game in progress.

Now this particular movie theater is part of a chain — the other Cinelounge Theater is on Sunset Boulevard in Hollywood. They do private bookings (what a fun place to party down) and besides the beer, wine, and gin and tonics, they sell Gourmet Organic Popcorn and champagne, and hats, socks and sweatshirts and the like.

For some of you on my list, the Hollywood extension may be closer than Tiburon, but let's not dwell on that.

We weren't really interested in the Trivia game and we were getting ready to high-tail it when he said that just a minute we'll see if we still have that movie, and if you'd like to see it, you can have a private showing in theater #2, but the heating system is down.

But we can supply you with some blankets.

So we said okay, and they gave us blankets. And I mean really nice, plush, soft, and warm blankets which kept us nice and cozy all evening.

Now, all the theater-type seats have been removed and replaced with a bunch of overstuffed sofas and chairs. Somewhat like the New Parkway Theater in Oakland, only a little more plush.

So we snuggled in and cozied up and watched "All Guys Are Losers" which was as crappy a movie as either one of us had ever seen. We would have walked out, but that would have been quite rude. And besides, (at least one of us) was enjoying our gin and tonic.

As I said, we had been there the previous Monday to see 'Triangle Of Sadness,' which was a strange, but very interesting movie.

Neither Carol or I cared that much for the ending, because nothing was tied up, but I'd give it an Excellent rating anyway, because it was fresh, and original, and because we were thinking about it and talking about it for days afterwards.

I suggest you watch the trailer online, then decide if you want to see it.

Do not, under any circumstances, waste your time on 'All Guys Are Losers' even if you can stream it for free, because that's an hour and a half that you'll never get back.

BABYLON

Starring Margot Robbie
And Brad Pitt

After Carol and I watched this movie, we went to get a hamburger and we _completely forgot_ about it. It went out of our minds totally.

And why was that, you might ask?

Not because it was boring. Even at a three hour running time it wasn't exactly boring.

It was more like _lame_. As in weak, thin, flimsy, insubstantial, and unconvincing.

It was like watching a three-ring-circus from 1952.

Only instead of the circus acts it was one huge party, with naked women, naked men, pseudo fornication, dancing, music, a jazz band, costumes, and general debauchery.

Kind of interesting to look at… but it'd be much better to have a compelling plot.

Let me paint a picture of the opening scene: This guy drives his big flatbed truck through what looks like a desert, only with a few orange trees and the title on the screen says 'Bel Air, California, 1920'. He stops to meet another guy (who apparently hired him to carry a couple horses to a movie site in the desert, but it turns out he wants to transport an elephant. So then we see them trying to tow the truck with the elephant in it up this steep dusty road and now one of the guys gets behind the back of the truck with the elephant and is pushing by hand (which is patently ridiculous in the first place) while throwing some kind of elephant food over into the space where the elephant is, and soon the elephant starts shitting — and I mean explosive diarrhea — which of course engulfs the guy who's pushing from behind.

And this went on for _way too long_.

It was more disgusting than funny. (I'm sure a lot of 12 year-old boys would have loved it).

So right then we realized: _"Oh. It's going to be that kind of a movie."_ And it was.

The story was about movie-making in the twenties during the silent film era. And I've gotta tell you a LOT of work went into this production. The were one-shot scenes with the camera moving through all kinds of party happenings, and there were scenes of movie backdrops one after another filming different types of pictures and there were hundreds of extras and all these different milieus, all signifying *nothing.*

Kind of interesting to look at, but…. *So what?*

It starred Margot Robbie as some kind of floozie/addict who was trying to make it in show biz despite her 'Eliza Doolittle' deportment. She actually did a very good job, such as it was. Again, so what?

Oh, and incidentally, Brad Pitt was in it as well. And he never changed his expression during the entire film, and seemed quite bored with the proceedings.

The guy who wrote this piece of crap also directed it. He should have found another director.

Way, way, WAY too many times in this thing, one character or another screams at the top of their lungs at someone or something. And I mean vein-popping sore-throat-inducing top-of-the-lungs screaming, which was very unpleasant.

I mean, it really became quite disturbing.

Also, all throughout the movie, when some one wanted someone to go away, it was never "Get outta here," "Take a hike," or "Get lost" — it was always *"GET THE FUCK OUTTA HERE!"*

Or get the fuck this or get the fuck that, or whatever. *SO* unnecessary.

They were obviously trying so hard to blow everyone's mind.

But the only ones whose minds will be blown are the aforementioned 12 year olds.

I'd advise you to stay the fuck away from this one.

Django, Unchained

A film by Quentin Tarantino

You know, it is very nice to have two historical films about the civil war released in late 2012. The first one, 'Lincoln', is a thoughtful and introspective tale about the life of Abraham Lincoln, that feels almost like a documentary. Daniel Day-Lewis creates a portrait of Lincoln that seems so genuine that I came away from the theater feeling like I had had a glimpse into the life of the *real* Abe Lincoln.

The other film, 'Django Unchained,' which takes place in Texas two years before the start of the civil war, is another significant historical tale which, in a way, parallels the Lincoln epic. It is the heart-wrenching tale of a freed slave, Django, played masterfully by Jamie Foxx, who, after gaining his freedom, decides to take revenge on his former oppressors, so he kills everyone in Texas. That is, every *white* person in Texas. And Mississippi, too. But, hey! They all deserved it!

I remember the elation I felt after seeing 'Inglorious Basterds.' Why, I had a smile on my face and a bounce in my step. Because the Jews had won! And here, again, is another feel-good theme, where the bad guys get theirs, and good! So once again, I walked out of the theater in a highly exhilarated mood.

It is always quite rewarding to see justice meted out to evil people. You might say that this movie appeals to our base instincts. Well, OF COURSE it does. Seeing malevolent white racists getting slaughtered unmercifully by Django? Fine by me.

There are also some very funny scenes, such as the one where a bunch of Ku-Klux-Klan types are riding out to kill the n---er and the n---er-lover and they stop and get in this long and involved discussion about how their hoods are ill-fitting and the fact that the eye-holes are not correct, and they can't see what they're doing, especially when they're riding at night, and one of them says, "Wait a minute. My wife spent the entire afternoon cutting eye-holes in these sacks and if the rest of you don't appreciate it, then the heck with it, I'm going home," and then riding off...

Now, it is very interesting indeed, the knack that Mr. Tarantino has for giving us a shower of blood when someone gets shot. Blood on the horses. Blood on the cactus. Blood on the walls, and on each other. It is funny, really. Not unlike a cartoon. Django becomes an expert shot, so he can gun down lots of people all at once and this is where the fun begins.

The people he kills are all dirty bastards anyway, so we feel no remorse, only justification. And with each shooting there is blood splattering everywhere, and plenty of it. When the going gets down and dirty, and Django needs to use some of the freshly killed corpses as a shield and bullets keep hitting the corpses and with each hit there is a new shower of blood, well, I'm sorry: It is SO over-the-top that all you can do is laugh. And it goes on and on and on. I'm still laughing.

You know, my second favorite movie of the year was 'Cabin In The Woods' (Favorite: 'Killer Joe'). One of the reasons 'Cabin' was so good, was that the blood letting was SO over the top that it was laugh-out-loud funny and eye popping all at the same time. And that's my idea of fun. Django has a similar tone. And I say, right on, Quentin. Way to go. A very nice piece of work, indeed.

I highly recommend this movie, especially to Quentin Tarantino fans. You will not be disappointed. Carol went with me, and though she has an aversion to blood-letting in movies, she actually liked this one.

Now, it is no "Reservoir Dogs" or even "True Romance," but in entertainment value, it is right up there. For me, one of the ways to gauge how much I liked a movie is when I ask myself "Would I go see it again?"

The answer: I can't wait!

ARGO

Starring Ben Affleck, John Goodman, Alan Arkin and others

Now that baseball season is over, and we've all come down from the high of Our Beloved Giants winning the World Series, I can get back to going to the movies regularly, and reporting on them to you. Case in point: 'Argo'. Or as they say in the movie, "Argo f--- yourself!", which is, by far, the ONE and ONLY clever thing about the entire production. Now, since 'Argo' is generating a lot of Oscar-contending chatter, I would like to set the story straight once and for all: If you want to see a movie where you know exactly what is going to happen from beginning to end, and there are no surprises whatsoever, then this one is for you.

Me, I want to be surprised. I want to see something new. Take me somewhere where I've never been. Please.

Disregarding one of my own cardinal rules, such as to never, ever, attend a movie where Ben Affleck is involved, I threw caution to the wind and went to see ARGO. I'm telling you, I knew it. But I got caught up in the talk. "Oh, it is really good... so-and-so said it was really good..." I asked my urbane and charming wife Carol to tell me who said this one was good. "Who is so-and-so, and who are the others?" (I would like to have a list of their names for future reference).

Sure, there was tension. There was also tension in 'Midnight Express,' which was a brilliant piece of work.

And, I might add, there was tension in every other movie depicting the *We're-Trapped -In-A-Foreign-Country-Where-They-All-Hate-Us-And-We've-Got-To-Sneak-Out-Right-Un der-Their-Noses-Phew-We-Made-It-That-Was-Close-Wasn't-It?* theme that has been made before and since. But in the rest of these movies, we had the benefit of *not knowing what was going to happen*. In ARGO, we know from the beginning how it is going to turn out. So I could have spent the time doing a crossword puzzle. Or sleeping. Or stapling my fingers to a board. All activities that wouldn't be quite as boring as having to sit though this drivel.

Sometimes I think I'll never learn. Or maybe it is just hoping beyond hope that for once a Ben Affleck movie would be good. But nope, his perfect record remains intact.

An interesting side note: At one point there is a shot, taken outside, from ground level, of Alan Arkin and John Goodman walking away while engaged in conversation. Now, how can I say this in nice way? Oh, I guess I can't. But John Goodman is as big as a house trailer. A double wide. I don't know what that boy has been eating, but it appears he's gone back for seconds.

The Armstrong Lie

Documentary by Alex Gibney

This is a terrific documentary about the Tour de France, and is very interesting and informative.

For instance, did you know why they say that the Tour de France is the most grueling event in all of sports?   It's because it entails riding up and down steep, winding mountain roads through the Swiss Alps, it takes three weeks to complete, and is 2,200 miles long.

No wonder drugs are involved.
Here's the deal: It appears that _everyone_ who competes in the Tour de France is using Performance Enhancing Drugs of one kind or another, period.

You know, I had written a long, involved review, spelling out every sleazy thing Lance Armstrong stooped to, with lists of every dope dealer he had ever known, along with the publicists, scientists, doctors, phlebotomists, and chemists that were on his payroll, but it was _boring!_

This movie is not boring.

Documentarian Alex Gibney set out to film an uplifting story about a great athlete's comeback from cancer. He ended up discovering that Lance Armstrong was doping from the very beginning, while lying voraciously. Gibney shows us what kind of guy Lance Armstrong really is, as he throws friend and foe alike under the bus, and commits the most atrocious lies in the history of sports.

Hence the title.

He has been banned from competing in any professional sport for life, which is fitting.

Now, he did raise a lot of money for cancer research, which
may be his only saving grace.

But, like Pete Rose, he manipulated everything, including
the timing of his confession, to his own benefit. Just as
everything else he has ever done in his life, it is completely
self-serving.

Fascinating documentary. Shows in great detail all the
methods they used to cheat. Not the least bit boring.

Muscle Shoals

There's no accounting for taste. That goes for everything. You might not care for peanut-butter and mayonnaise sandwiches, but I love 'em. Believe it or not, there *are* people who don't like chocolate ice cream. And it goes without saying that my music may not be your music. Which is fine.

Knowing all this, I would like to say that this is one of the best music documentaries I've ever seen. I *highly* recommend it.

It's about Muscle Shoals, a little town in the northwest corner of Alabama that has shaped the history of popular music. Famous since the sixties for the 'Muscle Shoals Sound', this terrific documentary is about the mystique behind the music made there, and the studio that has produced some of the finest R&B, rock, and country for years.

It is also the story of Rick Hall, who founded 'FAME' studios there and is quite a fascinating guy in his own right. And, it is a film about the 'Swampers', the legendary group of studio musicians who played back up on all this fabulous music.

But really, it's a documentary with a bunch of the coolest songs we've ever heard. Classics.

You'll see some of the greatest musicians in history, doing their thing. Including people like Buffalo Bill Jordanaire, Blind Willie Saucer Eyes, and Chief Sammy Treejump, to name a few.

Hey, wait a minute, Screamin', you just made up those names, didn't you?

Oh. I guess you were paying attention after all.

Seriously, this is about Rhythm & Blues, baby! And Rock, and Soul, and Country.

Some of the featured artists (really) include Clarence Carter, Etta James, Aretha Franklin, Wilson Pickett, Percy Sledge, Paul Simon, Bono, Steve Winwood, Jimmy Cliff, Mick Jagger, Keith Richards, Alicia Keyes, and Greg Allman.

This will bring back a bunch of memories. It has one of the best sound tracks I've ever heard. I didn't want it to end.

We saw it at the Rafael theater in San Rafael which has a great sound system. I suggest you do the same. You won't be sorry.

Blue Is The Warmest Color

One thing about foreign films is that they give a glimpse into what life is like in another culture. This is the coming-of-age story of Adele (the main character's name) played by Adele Exarchopoulos, who no one but the most resolute movie goers have ever heard of.

This is a beautiful, tender and touching love story about Adele and her first experiences with love and sex and her transition into womanhood. The acting is superb.

It is also very disturbing in some ways.

As the movie opens it shows the family at dinner. Eating spaghetti and sipping wine, there are quite a few *very close* close-ups of the mother, father, and daughter just eating and drinking, and not saying much. Funny how Carol and I saw that scene. I thought it was a very touching scene, with the mother glancing at the daughter, not saying anything, but smiling at her in the way that a loving and *accepting* (nurturing) mother would do. Carol thought it showed how alone they all were. In other words, no one was saying anything, they were all in their own worlds. Interesting.

Adele is a high school senior when the movie begins. It shows her in a variety of different *vignettes* of French life. In class, discussing philosophy, the classics, and great poetry. We see her at home with her family as described above, and with her high school homies talking crudely about sex, as 17-year-olds will do. Later we see her marching in some kind of a protest, then hanging in bars. Nice illustrations of French life.

As the story unfolds, Adele discovers she is attracted to a woman and eventually they enter into a great love affair. This is where the movie takes an uncomfortable turn. It is the sex scenes, which are really over done. They are way too graphic, and far too long. I swear, the first scene between the two women must've lasted 15 minutes! I must say that both of these women have beautiful bodies, so our prurient interests were somewhat satisfied, but still...

Listen, I am not a prude, by any stretch of the imagination. But, come on!
There are certain things that are none of my business! I don't know about
you, but I find myself getting a little embarrassed when actors start taking off
their clothes, going into heavy make-out sessions, and eventually *doing it.* I
don't think we need to see every detail of the love-making in *any* movie.

It used to be that these things were *hinted* at. They'd show a hotel, or a bed,
or a bedroom door, and a couple making googly eyes at each other, then
close the door, and fade to black. Allow us to use our imaginations.
Nowadays, they take you not only into the bedroom, but in any other
conceivable place that anyone could think of for the actors to take off all their
clothes and make hot, sweaty love, resulting in howling, screaming orgasms.

Let me tell you: If you were filming a lesbian-themed pornographic movie
you could just take the love-making scenes from this movie and you would
need nothing else. Because it shows everything and I mean everything and
in great meticulous detail. And I mean everything. My goodness.

Is this what it's come to? I guess so.

I believe director Abdellatif Kechiche wanted to make this as real as
possible, and if so, he did a great job. Close-ups, close-ups and more
close-ups in almost every scene. Several different camera angles shooting
the same quiet scene. And everything *was* very real, including the sex.
Which also caused the movie to be about THREE HOURS LONG! I was
getting bed sores, for crying out loud.

The bottom line: Although it was a very touching movie and the acting was
superb, it was WAY too long, and had WAY too much of the
none-of-our-business stuff for my taste.

I would welcome comments from any of you who have seen it, or from those
who haven't.

The Wolf of Wall Street

Starring
Leonardo diCaprio
Jonah Hill
Margot Robbie

One of the reasons we went to see this movie is because it was directed by Martin Scorsese. Yes, *that* Martin Scorsese. The one with the credentials: Taxi Driver, Raging Bull, Goodfellas, Mean Streets, The King of Comedy, and more. All of these films right up there as first-rate cinematic achievements, in my book. All of them great, all of them *real*.

Not to mention the fact that some critics are touting it as the *Next Best Thing*.

So we went in with high expectations.

Here it is in a nutshell: The damn thing is like a three-hour cartoon. Definitely an adult cartoon, but a cartoon nonetheless. There is so much swearing and debauchery and drug taking that it is absolutely ridiculous. This one makes the excesses of Al Pacino in Scarface look like Mary Poppins.

There were at least two older couples that walked out in the first 20 minutes or so, I assume it was because of the swearing and the sex. Could they have been older than this couple? I donno, but we certainly stuck it out.

Don't get me wrong. The acting is terrific, and it was pretty exciting for a while. There is a lot of funny stuff, and it is mostly pretty interesting for the first hour and a half or so, but then the story peters out and it just sort of becomes scene after scene of overindulgence and decadence. Except there are still a few funny scenes and some funny lines.

And some really stupid, over-the-top (even *cartoonish-wise*) scenes. But some folks were laughing, so you'll have be the judge.

There are so many prostitute/nudity scenes and boyfriend/girlfriend and husband/wife sex scenes, and so much drinking, coke snorting, profanity laced diatribes, and qualude popping to go along with the multitudes of stunningly beautiful *naked* women throughout the entire movie, that, well, it'll keep you glued to the screen.

I realize this may get some of you out there for tomorrow's matinee, and I certainly understand.

Leonardo plays a stock broker, actually a super salesman, and his spiel starts to get boring after the first ten times. By the time the movie gets into it's third hour, and he has degenerated into a shady Wealth Seminar host, I personally didn't need to hear him revving up the troops any more.

Some have suggested that this is a great work, to be ranked with some of the best Scorsese movies. To that I would say, *"They're entitled to their opinions, no matter how stupid they are."*

To me, it's not even close.

Bad Grandpa

Starring
Johnny Knoxville
Jackson Nicoll

Now remember, folks: This is the same Johnny Knoxville of 'Jackass' fame. So you kind of have an idea the direction this movie takes. Obviously, it isn't for everyone. You know, scatological humor, fart jokes and a lot of slapstick type gags *a la* the Three Stooges.

Just as obviously, there are a bunch of lame jokes. You've got to expect that in any movie that's billed as a comedy. Some funny stuff, and some lousy stuff.

For my money, the funny stuff in this one far outweighed the lame stuff.

As a matter of fact, there are several *side splitters,* and I am not kidding. I am telling you, at one point I was laughing so hard I seriously thought I was going to break a rib. And there were several more laugh out loud and keep on laughing long after the scene is over, and then start thinking about it again on the drive home and start laughing all over again.

Now, that's my kind of movie!

There's a kid actor named Jackson Nicoll (how old is he anyway, about eight?) who plays opposite Johnny Knoxville and steals the show. He's worth the price of admission.

Juvenile? Sure. Unsophisticated? Of course. But if you want to have a few laugh-out-loud moments, and a couple laugh-until-your-guts-hurt moments (and who can't use those), then this one is for you.

I'm still laughing.

As I said, this type of movie will not be appealing to some.

To those of you to whom it will appeal: I think you know who you are.

Inside Llewyn Davis
A film by the Coen Brothers

This one is about a starving folk singer in the sixties who is trying to make it and just *can't*. He doesn't have a place to live, he just has his guitar, and everything he does goes bad.

You know, it's funny how two people can go to the same movie and have totally different reactions.

Carol loved it. She said she could easily have stayed through two more hours of it. She thought it was a wonderful movie, a lovely and very real depiction of a melancholy situation and a melancholy person.

The movie opens with Llewyn Davis singing in some Greenwich Village sixties-style coffee house and at that point Carol leaned over to me and said *"He has a very sweet sounding voice, don't you think?"* But I didn't hear her because I was *already* trying to suffocate myself with a plastic bag that I had taken some cookies out of.

I <u>hated</u> it from the above-mentioned opening refrains to the closing credits.

Being by Joel and Ethan Coen, you'd expect a few laughs. I mean after all, don't they do comedy? But there aren't really any laughs. One reviewer said it was funny, but then again, he's a moron. Could be it's a 'dark' comedy.

Actually, there was one laugh that I got out of this one, but it was at an inappropriate time. It was when our lead character flips out and F-U's an old woman who has been nice to him. I guess that was my own personal reaction to hating the movie. I wanted someone to be hurt, or to suffer, just as I was suffering by having to sit through this crap.

Oh, there was one good part. One. It was when our lead character, Llewyn Davis, sang in a trio with a couple other guys in a take off called "Please Mr. Kennedy, I Don't Wanna Go" or something like that. Sort of a parody of "Please Mr. Custer" with a little bit of "Get Charlie Off the MTA" thrown in, about being shot into space. That was very good, and the only time in the entire hour and 45 minutes that I was entertained.

Other than that, it was as depressing a movie as I have ever had the misfortune to sit through. Nothing works out for this guy, and I mean *nothing*. It's like he's Midas's opposite twin, as his horrible, angry, and hateful ex-girlfriend says to him at one point.

Geez, just thinking about it again makes me depressed.

This one made 'Nebraska' seem like 'Yellow Submarine'.

HER

Starring Joaquin Phoenix

Both Carol and I figured there must have been a mistake. A misprint. A typographical error. I mean, how could this be? This piece of crap is nominated for best picture? Unbelievable.

You want to go see a movie where nothing happens? This is it. Not only does nothing happen, it happens to an inept klutz of a loser of a geek of a nerd who you can easily hate about five minutes into the movie and absolutely detest by the time it's over.

Wait, here's an idea: Let's go on a two hour tour of the morgue, and turn off all the lights and close all the boxes. Which still would be infinitely more interesting than this clunker.

I sat through it because it's my job. I did it for you. Plus, I was hoping something would happen. But, no. Nothing did. Everything was exactly the same through the entire stupid movie.

You all know it's about a guy who has a relationship with an operating system, right? And that it's the voice of Scarlett Johansson, right?

Well, so what?

It is really about someone who is the biggest dork you ever saw. Who can't relate to people so he relates to a computer.

Now, I will say that Joaquin Phoenix does a great job, but in the end, who cares? I mean, could something happen? Other than nothing?

And I am not kidding, it is the same from start to finish. Can you say static? How about *BORING?* Please. The character played by Joaquin Phoenix is such a stumblebum, and so lifeless, characterless, and insipid I wanted to scream.

I'm sure that this is exactly what they had in mind when they made this movie. They did it on purpose. To have a guy, who is so obviously dull witted and socially inept that the only thing he can relate to is a computerized being. Plainly, they had to accentuate the geekiness. Well let me tell you, they got that right. He is absolutely the nerdiest, geekiest dipshit you could ever imagine.

Just the thought of him makes me want to puke.

From boredom. Absolute and total boredom, frustrating boredom, thwarting every attempt to have *anything* happen, or to show any signs of life. Other than nothing. Or, I should say, the same stupid crappy meaningless existence with a fricking machine that no *alive* human being could possibly relate to because, even though it is the voice of Scarlett Johansson (which the makers of the movie have touted to no end), that doesn't matter at all, because it is just a voice! And soon, you forget it's Scarlett Johansson and it doesn't matter anyway, because in the movie, this guy doesn't know who Scarlett Johansson is!

If you think about it, they could have used the voice of Minnie Pearl. Or Eleanor Roosevelt. Or Dorothy Kilgallen for that matter, and it shouldn't have made any difference.

But therein lies the rub. It would have made a difference, because we are all picturing, at least subconsciously, Scarlett Johansson. But subconsciously picturing Scarlett Johansson is still not enough to stave off the screaming boredom that exudes from every frame of this film.

It was kind of interesting how the computer voice (Scarlett) grew and blossomed and eventually dumped him. But none of that matters because this damned thing is so f---ing boring and Joaquin Phoenix is so f---ing boring that I wanted to kill myself, really. No, I take that back. I wanted to kill him.

There were exactly six, count 'em, six other people at the screening we attended.

We saw it at the Four-Star theater on 24th and Clement in the City. Neither Carol nor I had been there in years and one of the most interesting things about this particular movie going experience... No, let me rephrase that: *THE most interesting thing about this particular movie going experience, and, as a matter of fact, the ONLY interesting thing...* was that the aisle was all lit up with a string of red lights going down each side as we headed toward the exit. It was really cool. Looked kind of like a depiction of a runway from the pilot's view on a computer.

Had we known what a stinking pile of garbage this movie was, we would have used it much earlier.

The Equalizer

With Denzel Washington

Man, this one looked good in the previews! You could just tell it was a great 'revenge' movie with Denzel taking care of the bad guys in his own inimitable way.

Sorry to say, it is quite disappointing.

First of all, how old is Denzel these days? 59? Not exactly a spring chicken. And he's got a middle-aged pot belly to go with it.

Remember those old Charles Bronson movies? Death Wish I, II, III, IV, and V? When he was an ex-cop going out and removing 'evil' people from the planet. On a one-man crusade to rid the world of all the slimeball-dirtbag-pimps and the like.

Well Charles Bronson was an old sucker as well, and it was kind of funny. He'd be all *"I'm kicking some ass right here and now.."* and he'd be in a tank top, and the loose skin on the backs of his arms would be flopping all over the place.

Not a good look. And not exactly credible.

This one reminded me of that. Yep. Denzel. *Old.* Kicking the asses of five or six guys in a room, all of them armed to the teeth with knives and guns, and he breezes through it like some caped crusader. Only he's an... an.... *Old Guy!*

I don't care. You can be the baddest mo-fo in the room, but when you're SIXTY, uh, sorry. It doesn't fly.

It could have been fun, but it was lame. The first scene of him taking out five or six guys was fun, but from there on out, it was boring as hell.

Stupid story, and completely unbelievable. They set it up so there's no question who the bad guys are (they all have serious body tattoos) and it is very clear from the beginning who the good guys are. Denzel and his homie, who both work at Home Depot (*Oh, sure*). Why does he work there? Because, well, who knows? Never did explain that.

And they portray him as a very kind unassuming guy who is in the middle of reading the top 100 classics like The Old Man and The Sea, by Chuck Norris. *haha*

Then, of course, a young girl gets manhandled by a pimp and he springs into action. And you know the rest. He kills every bad guy right up the ranks all the way to the top.

This one is not for the squeamish. There are some violent scenes that are really over done. Geez. You've been smashing that guys face in for about five minutes, do you think that's enough?

If you are a Denzel fan, I wouldn't recommend this one. Because he's done some fine work. This is not a part of it.

See *'A History Of Violence.'* instead. An excellent movie. Don't waste your time on this one.

Birdman, or the Unexpected Virtue of Ignorance
with Michael Keaton and Edward Norton

Okay, we saw this a couple weeks ago, and didn't particularly care for it, but I wanted to think about it for awhile and try to figure out what I had missed, because everyone else in the known universe is saying this is some kind of 'great' movie.

Well, I thought about it for a time, and I realized what I had missed: Going to a *good* movie.

So I didn't change my review at all. And here it is:

Esoteric, self-indulgent crap. This is a movie about actors, acting. And attempting to bore us to tears, and succeeding.

It stars Michael Keaton as a washed up actor trying to bring a broadway play to life and resurrect his career in the process. Now, I really like Michael Keaton, and even in this pretentious garbage there were a few scenes that were semi-interesting. But overall, this is one big piece of nothing.

Tons and tons of esoteric dialogue signifying naught.

Edward Norton comes on and plays himself, I'm sure. In other words, a raging, smug, condescending actor who is very good, but is so self-centered and uncaring about anyone but himself that he thinks he can do anything he wants, and he does.

Which causes huge blow-out arguments and fights between his and Michael Keaton's characters. You know, when I look back on this one, the main thing that comes to mind is a couple of middle aged actors screaming at one another.

Not at all pleasant.

It is billed as a comedy, but there were no laughs.

What am I missing here?

The only bright spot was Zach Galifianakis in a serious role as Keaton's right hand man, but his was really just a bit part.

Emma Stone plays Keaton's grown daughter who is a recovering addict and who is pissed at the world. Oh, yeah, this is just what I need to cheer me up; another unpleasant ex-junkie.

Many critics are giving this one a huge thumbs up.

So, I ask again: What the hell am I missing?

Gone Girl

Well, we finally went to see this one. Wanted to see what all the hubbub was about.

Didn't have a clue as to what kind of a movie it was, all we knew was that lots of people were talking about it and it was like the top box office draw for the week. Or month. Or whatever.

A curious thing about it was that people were saying *"I didn't like how it ended."*

It is based on the best-selling book of the same name, but I didn't read it so the ending was just fine with me.

Now, I'm not going to tell you anything about the ending of course, but I will tell you that the movie is about Scott Peterson, to a degree, and Nancy Grace. And the media circus and the whole ugly business that goes along with a missing woman.

Only this Scott Peterson character is definitely not guilty. He is suspected of killing his wife, but we, the viewers, know he is innocent because although she is 'missing', we know where she is. She's right up there on the screen. Hiding out. She has concocted this fantastically elaborate plan to hide, to change her identity, to disappear from her entire life.

Why? Because their marriage is falling apart, and they actually detest one another. And she wants to frame him for her 'death.' There are lots of twists and turns.

It is actually very interesting, although as it rolls along, it certainly begins to strain the credibility. As a matter of fact, when I think about it in retrospect, it seems silly, far-fetched, even ridiculous.

But: it is quite well done. Stylish, interesting and fast paced, and it keeps your attention. There are a couple of *severe* surprises along the way, which I would love to tell you about, but then you wouldn't be surprised.

Now, not having read it, I'm wondering if those same surprises were in the book.

And here's another thing. We saw it around five or six days ago, and I already almost forgot about most of it. Does this mean it is not a memorable movie? Yes, it does.

To those people who didn't like the ending: How would you have preferred that it ended? How did it end in the book?

The Girl Who Walked Home Alone At Night

"The first Iranian Vampire Western ever made, Ana Lily Amirpour's debut basks in the sheer pleasure of pulp. A joyful mash-up of genre, archetype, and iconography, its prolific influences span spaghetti westerns, graphic novels, horror films, and the Iranian New Wave."

"Moody and gorgeous."

"Like being in a dream..."

Well, I don't know about you, but these reviews were enough to make me want to rush right out and see it, even though vampire movies and the entire vampire *genre* in general is way down on the bottom of my list. I showed these to Carol, and she thought, well, okay, must be good, so we went.

And I have got to tell you folks, *do not fall for the hype.* This must be a movie-makers movie. An esoteric film that only a critic who watches movies all day and all night could love.

It is a little different, I will admit.

But here's the deal: You take your David Lynch, you take your Sergio Leone, You take your who? Clint Eastwood? Yep, he would fit in here, because we are talking *SLOW*, folks. Great way to catch up on your sleep.

It is real nice to admire the old Sergio Leone spaghetti westerns for what they were, but my sweet bleeding Mary, they could sure drag out a scene. Same as David Lynch. He's done some great films, but this one reminded me of EraserHead. Too slow. Too brooding. Too surreal.

Clint Eastwood does the same thing, maybe because he starred in so many of those old spaghetti westerns, that is, drag a scene out, milk it for all it's worth, and then some.

My goodness, I do not need to see someone walking down the street for fifteen minutes.

Not saying anything.

In black and white.

Yeah, this film is dreamy, alright. As in snore fest.

Okay, so the 'girl' who is a vampire rides a skateboard that she unceremoniously steals from a young innocent boy.

Yes, she rides a skateboard.

And... and... and... *nothing.*

Well, there's a huge *"So what?"*

There is one great scene where she kills a disgusting pimp, other than that, the whole darn thing is ho-hum.

The male lead looks like a cross between James Dean and Sal Mineo right out of "Rebel Without A Cause." White tee shirt with the sleeves rolled up... Hey, we did that as kids in the... Uh-oh, do I have to say the *fifties* here? God, that was a long time ago.

But I digress. This thing is so dark, despairing, and silent! And slow. Oh wait, did I say that already?

I'm telling you, it was a chore to keep my eyes open.

I realize in my description here that it may sound good to some. But I'm telling you, unless you are an "art" movie lover, or... what? What word would fit here? Masochist? Insomniac?

It's enough to make an old codger scream.

Wolfpack

You know what this one is about, don't you? It's a documentary about these six brothers, who were spotted one day walking on the lower East Side of New York City, by a filmmaker from Mill Valley, CA. The reason they stood out is because they looked like the cast from Reservoir Dogs. Thin ties, white shirts, sunglasses, the whole bit.

So after talking with them, the filmmaker comes to find out that this is one of the first times they have all been outside. And looking into it further, she discovers that they've all been kept in their tenement home for their entire lives. Basically never going into the outside world from the time of their birth until sometime after the oldest is around 21 or so.

Their father, who was from Chile or Peru did all the grocery shopping and they were home schooled by their mother. They had an extensive collection of movies from which they gained their entire life experiences.

They play-acted entire scenes, and entire movies from what I could tell. Movies such as the aforementioned Reservoir Dogs, and Pulp Fiction and others. They had all kinds of props and costumes. So much fun seeing one of these guys with an afro wig playing the Samuel Jackson part from Pulp fiction opposite another brother doing the John Travolta role.

None of these boys had ever cut their hair until sometime during the filming of this movie.

The Dad was the driving force behind them never going out. He projected his own fears on the entire family, including the weak-willed mom, so there they all stayed. Sad situation, really.

Absolutely fascinating. A little slow at times, but an amazing story.

Jurassic Park II

As you may or may not know, this movie grossed something like a half *billion* dollars in its first weekend of release. Unfortunately, we contributed our share to that total as well.

Listen, have you seen the previews? Well then, you've seen the movie. Only difference is, is that in the actual movie, the dinosaur fights are longer. But what does that matter anyway? For one, you can't really tell the difference between the good dinosaur and the bad dinosaur. They both have those giant heads with thousands of teeth and those little teeny arms dangling from their chests.

Now, we weren't expecting much, and we got less.

From the very opening lines of this corny, pointless piece of crap we knew we were in for a special treat. As in cheese. As in cheesy.

I wanted to see dinosaurs. I wanted to be scared. I wanted to scream like a little girl, even. But no such luck.

Oh, there were dinosaurs, and they were real enough, but it seemed a little more like a painting that they got to move somehow. In the first Jurassic, there were some genuine startling moments, and some really scary scenes.

In this one... hiding under a truck? Sorry, that isn't getting it.

You know that dino-boy is going to kick the truck into the next county, and who gives a crap when he does? And another thing: if the leads in this movie were to get killed, that would have been a saving grace. As a matter of fact, we were actively rooting for the female lead to get hers.

Until later, of course, when she stripped down to her undershirt.

But none of that is either here nor there. We would have gotten the same charge out of it if it were in another language, or if it were a silent film. Because silence would have been better than the embarrassingly bad dialogue that those poor actors were forced to recite.

In any case, there was some kind of morbid fascination for me to go see this movie, and I'm glad I did.

There was one very short and quick scene that made me happy, made me giggle, and that was when a huge, and I mean HUGE, prehistoric fish-monster jumps out of the ocean and swallows a giant pterodactyl whole. As the enormous bird is being eaten, his tongue pops out of his head like one of those squishy-squeezy toys.

Other than that, ho-hum.

You know, when there is a dinosaur fight, and these two behemoths are going at each other, and they knock down towers and sparks fly everywhere, then they do the same exact thing from a different angle, then again from another angle, knocking down towers and sparks flying.... Well, how many times can they do that without the audience starting to throw things at the screen? Answer: As many times as they want and it won't even matter.

I'm telling you, it was tedious.

Oh, well. Next week, San Andreas.

DEADPOOL

Starring Ryan Reynolds

As the opening shots come onto the screen, it's kind of hard to make out exactly what it is, because the camera is panning back as it is rolling ever so slowly. Almost like still shots. Soon we realize it is some kind of a vehicle in mid roll, with various things flying everywhere and people hanging all over it, mainly our hero. As the camera rolls back and the picture comes into focus, we see our hero with a firm grasp on a pair of undies, inadvertently giving someone a huge wedgie.

As all this is happening, the credits begin to roll. "Douchebag Productions Presents," it said. "A Film." Starring: "A Hot Chick." "A Very Bad Guy." "A Moody Teenager." And on and on... and produced by "A Bunch Of Asshats."

Now, obviously, this was my kind of movie.

Let me tell you, folks, this baby was HILARIOUS!

SO MANY one-liners. By everyone, all throughout the entire movie. Unbelievable. Our hero, Mr. Dead Pool, is talking like the old Popeye cartoons about half the time. As he goes about his business stabbing and killing people left and right, he's mumbling one-liners under his breath. *Very funny* one-liners.

Here's the gist of it: Our hero is a washed up Special Forces guy, who now just does favors for people. In other words, helps protect the innocent by hurting bad guys.

Then, he meets a hot chick and falls in love. That part took a little too long. Then, the bad guys get him and torture him, the end result of which is he becomes a very ugly, yet indestructible SuperHero.

Now, I didn't know this was a Superhero movie until about half way in. But that's what it turned out to be. In any case, this was the best Superhero movie I've ever seen.

Also the only one.

Some of the fights lasted a little too long, and the torture scene became a little much, but the wisecracks! Oh, baby, they just kept coming! My goodness, it was like a vaudeville routine with swearing.

Lots of attention to detail here, lots and lots of sight gags as well.

Loved it, loved it, loved it.

Can't wait to see it again!

Deadpool 2

With Ryan Reynolds, Josh Brolin

Listen, don't go and see this movie unless you want to laugh your ass off for almost two hours.

This is hilarious from start to finish. All kinds of laughs, including sight gags, slapstick, and lots of very contemporary, profanity laced, side-splitting humor.

From beginning to end, there is rarely a dull moment. Well, it gets a little repetitious with all the fighting, but the humor trumps everything. Non-stop sarcasm and ridiculously funny lines.

This is a lampoon of a 'Superheroes' movie, and it is dead on target. As in the first Deadpool, the hero (Ryan Reynolds) is a sarcastic, foul-mouthed ruffian of the highest degree.

In one part of the movie, they are looking for some super hero types to hire to go on a mission to save someone from something. So they're conducting interviews, asking them all what their super powers are. One fellow's super power is vomiting flesh eating acid.

So there are about 5 or 6 of them on this mission, and they all end up parachuting from a plane.

Our hero, Deadpool, gets hung up on a billboard, one of the guys gets electrocuted on high voltage lines, and the guy that vomits acid lands in one of those tree mulching machines but as he's being sucked in, another of the super-heroes tries to pull him out, but acid boy vomits on him, which of course eats half his body quickly and he dies.

And the rest of them all die in various ways before the mission begins.

Sound like your kind of humor?

It's mine *fer shur!* You know who you are.

Report back to me, please.

Hereditary

Starring Toni Collette, Alex Wolff, Milly Shapiro, Ann Dowd, Gabriel Byrne

It is my duty as a movie commentator to protect you from going to see bad movies.

This is a bad movie.

Do not waste your time.

What starts out as a promising, seemingly intelligent, well-acted (and in it's favor, it is well-acted) 'horror' film, devolves into a run-of-the-mill Stephen King type movie that becomes a boring study in inanity.

This isn't one of those jump out of your seat scary movies, it's more along the lines of 'Rosemary's Baby' scary. But it isn't really that frightening at all, and by the time the so-called scary parts begin to happen, your belief has long been suspended and the whole thing has grown ludicrous.

For the first half of the movie, it is quite engrossing. Very good, very interesting, and very well done. Then it takes a turn into inanimate objects moving on their own, jumps on into seances (really?) and goes downhill from there, until it becomes a bad parody of a horror film.

They try to piece it all together by tying the evil grandmother to some woman the mom meets in a parking lot, but none of that matters, because by that time you're thinking about who won the Giants game, or what time your dentist's appointment is next Tuesday.

In reference to this movie, there's a lot of talk about demonic possessions, cults and devil worship.

When 'The Exorcist' first came out, some people I know laughed at it. But not I. It scared the bejesus out of me, not because of the religious aspect, but because of what the human mind is capable of.

This ain't no 'Exorcist.'

I'm telling you, you'll be sorry.

Won't You Be My Neighbor

Starring Fred Rogers

The story of Mister Rogers, a fabulous documentary about a most unusual man.

Back in my day, we wouldn't have had anything to do with Mister Rogers. Why? Because we were way too macho. And he was the epitome of girliehood. Of square. Of everything we were uncomfortable with in a man.

Because we were infantile boys parading around as men. But that's a whole 'nother story.

Then one day, about 20 years in, a woman (wish I could remember who it was) who was raising kids overheard me making snide comments, and mentioned that all that may be true, but he is really good for kids.

So I started to see him differently. And, I like to think, *in my maturity,* I came to like him.

This heartfelt, touching, emotional documentary shows just what an extraordinary man he was, and what a positive influence he was on children for so many years, and it is absolutely delightful.

Never a dull moment in this moving portrait of a man who knew exactly what he was doing and how important it was and is to give children a positive view of themselves.

Highly recommended.

Battle Of The Sexes

Starring Emma Stone, Steve Carell, Bill Pullman, Sarah Silverman, and Elizabeth Shue

First of all, let me say that all of these actors did a great job with their parts. Emma Stone looked pretty much like the real Billie Jean King, and Steve Carell *was* Bobby Riggs. Fine job.

As for Sarah Silverman: She was amazing. Wow. That woman is a fine actress. Who knew?

Bill Pullman played former tennis star and the then-leader of the men's chauvinist pig movement. He was very good as well.

And it was nice to see Elizabeth Shue. Haven't seen her in a while. Does she get much work these days?

Now, as for the movie itself: Carol said that each time she woke up, she thought it was pretty good.

She was lucky. I couldn't get to sleep to save my life.

I'm telling you, all these people did their characters wonderfully.

And it bored me to tears.

About as exciting as watching paint dry.

If you go to see this one, you might like to bring your pajamas.

And a pillow.

And maybe a good book to read.

LA LA LAND

With Ryan Gosling
and Emma Stone

Oh.

My.

God.

You know, some movies start out okay, then bottom out later. Not this one. It hit bottom
before the credits started.

It started out on the L.A. freeway, with the camera panning down a long line of cars
locked in a traffic jam. In a minute a woman in one of them starts in singing, then gets
out of her car, still singing, then others join her, and the traffic jam becomes a set for
what is supposed to be a big song lalapalooza of some kind, but seems really strained
and pushed. It's like they wanted to open the movie with a big number, with people
dancing on top of cars and singing, and they did, but the music was not exactly catchy.
As a matter of fact, it was downright boring.

To be fair, there was some scattered applause in the theater audience when this first
number was over, so some people liked it.

But, please. Emma Stone? Wasn't she the same little bug-eyed actress who played in
that other dreadful movie opposite Michael Keaton? You remember, the one where
Keaton sprouts wings toward the end and flies away?

And Ryan Gosling? Who the hell is he, anyway? He is definitely NOT a singer, as was
apparent during the first two notes of the first song he was assigned to sing. I mean,
can you say embarrassing?

Another word about Emma Stone. She may not be a very good singer, but she can't
dance a lick.

I guess this was supposed to be a wonderful musical about life in L.A.

If they were serious about that, maybe they should have found some good music. Or
some stars who could actually sing?

What is it these days with people who can't sing being cast in singing roles? First it was Meryl Streep in Mama Mia, which was dreadful enough, but this one...

It is unbelievable, really, because Los Angeles is absolutely loaded with talent of every kind. So why, I ask you, would they settle for these two?

I'd love to tell you how the plot developed, or what, if any, good songs there were, but I ran screaming from the theater before the third song got started.

Good luck if you go to this one.

I, Tonya
With Margot Robbie

Okay, this one started out to be a real knee-slapper. Really. It was hilarious.
And it ended up funny. The final scene was great!

Margot Robbie does an excellent job as Tonya Harding.

They played up the 'trailer trash' bit to the nines. Tonya really had to
overcome a seriously red-neck upbringing to get to the pinnacle of the
ice-skating world. You've got to hand it to her for that.

But as the movie went on, and the physical and mental violence against her
by everyone she ever encountered, especially her own mother, really soured
me. There were funny parts as the story unfolded, but in between, Tonya
was getting pushed, slammed, slugged and bloodied by her moronic
boyfriend/husband, and emotionally and mentally tortured by her sadistic
and heartless mother, who wrote the book on 'How To Make Your Child Hate
You.'

You begin to understand why Tonya would think she deserves to be beaten
up all the time.

Hopefully, if you go, you'll be able to emotionally disconnect, which is what
Tonya had to do her whole life in order to carry on.

For me, it was hard to take. Funny, yes, but on the other hand a real
bummer.

So, go ahead. Go see it. See if I care.

All The Money In The World

With Michelle Williams, Christopher Plummer, and Mark Wahlberg

This is the story of J. Paul Getty III being kidnapped for ransom in Rome in 1973.

Here is a quick synopsis: *That's two hours of my life that I can never get back.*

Number one: Mark Wahlberg is getting as much work as Morgan Freeman these days, no? He seems to be in just about every other movie that's out. Unfortunately, he plays the same character in all of them: Mark Wahlberg.

Hey, Mark! Give it a rest.

Michelle Williams does a great job as the mother of 16 year old J. Paul III, and Christopher Plummer does equally well in his role as J. Paul Getty himself.

But the trouble is, *NO ONE CARES.*

Here you've got a bunch of Calabrese knuckleheads pitted against J. Paul senior, who happened to be a man with about as much compassion as a hub cap, then you add a few of J. Paul's lawyers, and Mark Wahlberg, and what have you got?

A study in monotony.

A tedious, banal, dreary, wearisome, uninteresting waste of time. As I said: Two hours I can never get back.

It was unfortunate that the party I was with wanted to stay, because I would have gone about 20 minutes in. As it was, I walked out to the concession stands several times and stared at the candy selections for a while.

We should have known the moment we drove into the parking lot, and it was just about empty.

Our next clue was when we entered the theater itself and there were about 5 others in attendance.

That would have been a good time to high-tail it.

But no. *Someone* made me stay.

Someone just had to see it through.

Someone, when it was all said and done, was almost as bored as I was.

Seriously, what about character development? Is that a concept that they don't bother with anymore? In this film, you see a 16 year old boy (who looks 22, btw) walking down the street and boom! He gets grabbed and thrown into a car and taken away.

Does anyone care? Of course not. We don't know this kid, we don't know anything about him. We don't know if he helps grandmothers across the street, or if he's a puppy killer. To us, he's just a blank face on the screen.

It used to be that in order to tell a story, you would need to explain what kind of a person this is, at least make them empathetic, so that the audience could care. What the heck happened to that concept?

There are some movies that have character development in spades: "The Celebration," a Dutch film from 1998 is a prime example. Which is why it is on so many peoples top-ten lists. All the Godfather movies as well. There are many, many movies in which, because of the way the story is told, we are made to feel empathy for the characters.

It seems like some folks in the movie business don't think that's necessary.

No wonder the theater was empty.

SILENCE

A Martin Scorcese film

There are some great directors out there, whose movies you go see automatically, no questions asked. Martin Scorcese, for me, is right up there at the top of the list. But he may have slipped down a few notches with this clunker.

I'm pretty sure the reason it was called 'Silence' is because when it was over, the other five people in the theater were all asleep.

It takes place in Japan in the early 1600's, obviously before the invention of soap. It's about these two white boys, I mean priests, who travel to Japan to preach the gospel and praise Jesus to the Japanese Christians. The *poor* Japanese Christians. The villagers. The ones who are still awaiting the invention of soap.

At that time, it was forbidden in Japan to be Christian, so they ordered all those suspected of being Christ lovers to put their foot on a woodcut of his image, thereby proving they were Buddhists. Most of them wouldn't do it, so they were subjected to torture or beheading.

Now, all of this may sound interesting, but I can assure you, it is not. This thing is so slow, and so murky, and half the time you can't understand what the Japanese bad guys are saying but it doesn't really matter, because halfway through the movie you stop caring. Or should I say you've given up trying to manufacture any empathy for the lead character.

I began to hope he'd get himself beheaded so we could just all go home. But, *NO*. This thing dragged on for another hour after we stopped caring.

No wonder everyone was asleep.

Don Jon

Starring
Joseph Gordon-Levitt
Scarlett Johansson
Julieanne Moore
Tony Danza
Glenne Headly
Brie Larson

One of the reasons I was a little reluctant to see this film, is because it is about a guy who is addicted to internet porn.

I was thinking: *Internet Porn?* That is a very private matter indeed (*wink wink, nudge nudge).*

But not to worry. It is all done with humor and class, and it is not dwelled upon. The quality of this movie far outweighs any uncomfortable feelings one may have about the subject matter.

It is far more a psychological, romantic, comedy/drama about relationships than a movie about porn.

The reason I listed every actor in this movie is because *everyone* in it is good.

The lead character, played by Joseph Gordon-Levitt (who also wrote and directed), is Jon Martello, a ladies' man, and kind of a modern-day John Travolta, straight out of Saturday Night Fever. He is terrific. Scarlett Johansson plays his sometime girlfriend, and she is wonderful as a controlling, Beautiful Individual Totally in Control of Herself. Tony Danza plays the Italian father figure in his wife beater T-shirt, in a role slightly reminiscent of Marlon Brando in 'Streetcar,' only with more colorful language. Glenne Headly is his wife, who is your standard *grandma-wanna-be* doting Mom, and Brie Larson is the sister who, in every single scene, has the same detached, bored expression as she is looking at her phone and texting.

Julieanne Moore is an older student going to the same night-school classes that Jon attends, who becomes friendly with him.

This is a good movie, folks.

The setting alternates between the night club scene, the Catholic church (mainly the confessional box), and the nice little family home in the Italian New Jersey neighborhood.

While sex, and addiction to internet porn seem to be the overriding themes, this is far more a theme of relationships. But I already said that.

Believe me, it is all very tastefully done. You have all seen more sex, more graphically depicted, during your average run-of-the-mill movie-going experience.

This one is touching (*No, not that kind of touching, get your mind out of the gutter*), heartwarming, and very funny.

There is never a dull moment. Now, I don't like to give away the story lines, or divulge plots. I more just like to let you folks know whether or not a movie is good or bad.

This one is Excellent with a capital E!

I *highly* recommend it.

The Disaster Artist

Starring James Franco, Seth Rogan

The main reason I am writing this is to contradict another movie critic. That would be Mick Lasalle, of the SF Chronicle, who says *"…this picture is the funniest movie of the year in a year of funny movies."*

He calls it *"Side-splitting."*

My first question would be: *OMG, WHAT THE HECK WAS HE SMOKING? Or shooting? Or drinking? Or all three?* Whatever it was, I want some.

I'm sorry, this movie was not funny.

I am a big fan of both James Franco and Seth Rogan, and I'm sure they had lots of fun making it. i think I might have laughed, sort of, maybe once.

Side-splitting? My goodness. I don't get it.

Maybe it is some kind of a movie industry inside joke.

Based on a true story, it is about the making of possibly the worst movie of all time, entitled 'The Room.' Made in around 2002, this movie was self financed and directed by a mysterious, wealthy, and bizarre person named Tommy Wiseau.

Practice pronouncing all your words without letting your tongue touch the roof of your mouth. Now, if you can do that, you have the whole movie in a nutshell. Because that is how James Franco speaks for the entire film. As it began, and he first started talking like that, I figured, okay, that's stupid, but it can't go on. But it did, and never stopped.

Now, I'm sure that depicted how the real Tommy Wiseau spoke.

But here's the thing: *WHO CARES??*

I would really like to hear from anyone else who has had the misfortune to have seen this to try to find out what I'm missing.

Where To Invade Next

Go see Michael Moore's latest entitled, Where To Invade Next.

This is a terrific film, folks. Funny, inspiring, educational, enlightening, touching and profound. All done in a light hearted way. It gives a nice perspective on certain customs in European countries versus those in the USA.

The premise is that he goes to a few other countries, mostly European countries, to find things that they do better than us. Then he'll plant an American flag, and claim the idea for the U.S. of A. Well, that is kind of silly, but the fact is is that he finds some very interesting things around there in some o' them countries.

Such as 7 week paid vacations every year, an extra months' pay at Christmas time, gourmet food served for public school lunches, completely free college tuition, even for foreigners, grade schools that have no homework, and bankers who are punished for ripping off consumers by being put in jail. What a concept.

You may want to move to Italy after seeing this one.

It isn't so much a put-down of our ways here, but more a celebration of some of the great things that are standard in other countries.

Very enjoyable. Of course it's slanted. Michael Moore never claimed to be objective. If you are a Republican, or you ever voted for George W. Bush, you probably won't get as much out of this as some of us do.

I HIGHLY recommend this one. LOVED it.

It isn't ALL fun and games. There are some horrible comparisons to Nazi Germany and the systematic genocide and incarceration of blacks in this country. But only as a lesson to remember your history so it can't be repeated.

All in all, the best thing he's done yet.

The Big Short

Excellent movie, folks.

Fast paced and entertaining the whole way.

Now, you wouldn't think that a movie about banking and real estate loans and the stock market could be anything other than a snooze fest. As a matter of fact, neither would I.

But you don't have to know a hedge fund from a goldfish to enjoy this one. It's the personalities of the actors who make this a great film. Also the way it's presented.

When they think that something needs explaining, they basically stop the movie, look right into the camera, or have other interesting people do it, and give a short explanation of what it all means. Quite clever and very entertaining.

Not a dull moment here.

Go see it.

The Hateful Eight
A Quentin Tarantino film

Billed as 'Quentin Tarantino's Eighth Movie' (by him no doubt), which doesn't seem *too* egotistical, but that's neither here nor there.

Not everyone is a Quentin Tarantino fan. Some people find his movies rather distasteful. Crude, violent, hard to watch. Too real. All the reasons why I think he's the best film maker of this generation.

I've been a fan for quite some time. Ever since Reservoir Dogs. Besides that one, he has made several movies that belong on top ten lists, period. Inglorious Basterds, Django Unchained, Pulp Fiction, Jackie Brown. He also wrote True Romance and Natural Born Killers. Man! That is quite an impressive resume.

Now, here's the story on Hateful Eight: It has a little touch of the directing style of Clint Eastwood. You know, let's drag it out a little just to make sure the audience *gets* it. Maybe because the movie was shot in 70mm, Quentin figured he needed to do scene after scene of the frozen tundra, the grey skies, the snow, ice, etc etc.

Okay, we get it. It's cold.

Brrr.

But maybe us die-hard Tarantino fans are a little restless. Waiting for the mayhem that we have come to know and love. Maybe we're impatient; we want to get to the nitty gritty. But of course there always needs to be some character building. I mean, we need to know who we're dealing with, right? And character building is definitely one of Quentin's strong suits.

Kurt Russell stars as a hard guy, a bounty hunter who is taking a woman to Red Rock to be hanged. He's a gruff talker, and every word out of his mouth is a threat of some kind, delivered in what could be described as 'Professional Wrestler Gibberish.' There was some comic relief with his character along the way, but mostly it was him swearing and threatening to kill everyone if things didn't go his way. That got a little tiring. As a matter of fact, I found myself hoping someone would shoot him.

But there was a lot more to this film than Kurt Russell talking in a gravelly voice. There
were all the rest of the characters. Some of the cast of Reservoir Dogs (Tim Roth,
Michael Madsen) were here, plus Samuel L. Jackson, and Bruce Dern, of all people.

This movie was told in 'Chapters', conveniently spelled out at the top of the screen.
After about four chapters of character building, I was beginning to think this one was
going to be a dud. Because as much as we all like the hard guys, if it isn't backed up
with action, then why bother?

As in "Money talks, bullshit walks."

So when the trademark mayhem began, that havoc that we know and admire Mr.
Taranatino for, our patience through the first few chapters was rewarded. Because it not
only tied the whole story together, but the violence was total, and complete.

He came through again. We got our payoff, in spades.

When judging a movie, the question you might ask yourself is "Would I see it again?"

Answer: I can't wait.

Shtar Warsh, Inshtallment Sheven
(The Forshe Awakensh)

Well, we finally got around to seeing Star Wars.

This is the movie that has generated nearly 2 BILLION dollars in world wide revenues. Wow. Is that amazing, or what?

We went to the Grand Lake theater in Oakland to see it on the BIG screen. But when we got there we were funneled down into a theater about the size of boxcar.

Note to self: Hey, Bill, did you think of checking it out beforehand?

It probably would have been nicer on the big screen because of all the special effects. But in the end, it all boils down to the age old question: Does Anyone Give A Rat's Ass? Or, D.A.G.A.R.A.

Oh, some of the special effects were amazing, the actual BIGNESS of it all, and the weird non-human characters and strange animals. You know, the old bar scene with all the otherworldly beings? Which was the only interesting thing in the movie, and was over and done with in about 30 seconds.

But, no one really gives a horse flop.

Take Darth Vader. Please. In this installment he has a severe anger management challenge. When things don't go his way, he breaks up an instrument panel on his space ship.

Darth! Get it together, man!

(D.A.G.A.R.A.)

Early on, the evil forces rounded up a bunch of what appeared to be innocent bystanders and slaughtered them on the spot. Guess they needed to show who the bad guys were. But really, we could have figured it out since they were all dressed like nazis. Only thing missing was the swastikas.

Meanwhile the good guys were all trying to figure out how to overcome insurmountable odds and blow up the death star of the bad guys and then, about a third of the way in, old Harrison Ford, the original Han Solo, showed up. And I do mean old. I guess that was supposed to be cool or something.

But really, no one cares. No one gives a steaming cow pie.

And later in the movie, the original Pricness Leah shows up: That's right, Carrie Fisher. OMG, big mistake. Listen, she wasn't exactly a beauty queen when she was young, and aging has not been kind.

And besides, no one gives a flying crap at all.

I was wondering when Jabba the Hut was going to drop by. At least that might have been enough to keep us awake.

At some point during the insurmountable tedium, I noticed that the wall of the theater was inscribed with a bunch of Egyptian hieroglyphics. Very cool. I got busy deciphering while up on the screen they were having fights of every kind.

If they weren't sword fighting with light sabers, they were flying around in personal mini-rocket ships shooting at each other, and when they weren't doing that, they were killing each other with rifles and pistols.

But in the end, I'm still wondering how anyone could possibly give a ribbon of snot about any of this...

The Revenant

This is the one that won Best Picture at the Golden Globes, and also got Leonardo DiCaprio the Best Actor award.

I'm sorry, I'll take 'Brooklyn' any day.

Based on true events, this is the story of frontiersman Hugh Glass, who, after being attacked by a bear, is left for dead by his comrades.

It is about misery, pain, and hardship. Trials and tribulations. Never ending difficulty. Unspeakable trauma. Torment and fear. And unceasing agony.

Unfortunately, the one suffering the unceasing agony was the viewer, because the trials and tribulations just *wouldn't quit.*

Each new misery seemed to eclipse the last. If he wasn't crawling, severely wounded, through the snow, he was being attacked by angry Pawnees, or falling off a cliff, or being caught in raging currents.

All which would have been just fine, but they just didn't know when to stop! Did they need to include every nightmare, every trauma, every hardship he ever endured until it became an agonizing wait for the damn picture to *get on with it?* As in *get to the point?!* Enough with the ordeals!

I mean, how many ordeals can we take?

There were about an hour too many here.

Oh, it got off to a great start. It was as tense and gripping as any film I've ever seen. For the first hour. I'm not kidding, I had a knot in my stomach.

And for that first hour, it was a great movie. Then, they added another ordeal. And another. And several more. And some of the themes were repeated, such as crawling, wounded, through the snow. And crossing the plain, and being taken by rapids.

While each of the tribulations were nerve racking and fearsome, after a while we just needed them to *wrap the damn thing up!*

It started getting stale (just like this review), which screwed up what should have been a great movie.

Would I see it again? Not on your life. It was about one light year too long.

Listen, it is not my intent to dissuade people from seeing this movie. This is just my own personal take on it.

Who knows? I'm sure there are lots of folks who will enjoy each and every hour.

Brooklyn

Now that baseball season is good and over, I've tried and tried to catch up on my movies. We've seen a bunch in the past few weeks, as a matter of fact. But none of them did much at all for me, because for me, I want to be *taken*. I want something new or fresh or unseen, and if I don't get that, I want to be moved. Know what I mean?

That is, until we saw 'Brooklyn.'

Saw **"The Night Before"** with Seth Rogan. Why? That's what I was asking myself after being screamingly bored for the entire hour and a half I wasted watching this piece of crap. I know what I was thinking. I was thinking **"This Is The End,"** one of the most fabulous, original, cleverest, funniest, filthiest and actually heartwarming movies to be released this year. The Night Before was with Seth Rogan and a some of his homies and I was thinking *"Okay! More great Hi-Jinks by these very funny boys!"* But I should have known better.

Also saw **Spotlight, The Letters** (reviewed earlier), **Bridge Of Spies, Spectre, Trumbo**, and **Janis**, none of which *moved* me. Oh, some of them were good. For instance Bridge Of Spies really took us. It was very well done, tense from start to finish. And **Spotlight** was quite a piece of work as well. This was the one about the Boston Globe reporters uncovering the wide-spread pedophile catholic priest scandal. The most interesting part of this movie for me was when it was over and the credits started rolling not a single person got out of their seat. Everyone just sat in stunned silence, because as a final gesture, the filmmakers listed, on the screen, all the dioceses where priests had molested young boys, and there were hundreds and hundreds of them all over the world. Shocking, to say the least.

Spectre was absolute garbage. The opening scene was exiting, as in most James Bond movies, but we had seen the damn thing in previews and advertisements so many times it was boring already. In one of the final scenes we see Christoph Waltz, as the villain, lying on the floor, with some kind of gory wound on the left side of his face, giving his final speech and I swear to god it looked like some kind of cartoon. As did most everything else in this complete and total embarrassment.

Trumbo was kind of okay, I guess, but there was definitely no feeling there. The guy who played Dalton Trumbo was cold and calculating and full of zippy one-liners, and was completely devoid of human emotion. Quite forgettable, in my opinion.

And I absolutely couldn't get worked up about **Janis**. Man, that girl was on a crash and burn mission from childhood. It's hard to watch such a self destructive being unfold in front of our eyes into their ultimate fate. Sad, sad life.

Then we saw **Brooklyn**. An excellent movie. A lovely film. Very well done. This is a story about a young Irish lass in the fifties who gets a job in a Brooklyn department store and sails from Dublin the U.S. all alone. She lives in a boarding house with a bunch of other Irish girls and this movie really captures what it was like back then, with the house mother watching over all the girls, dispensing rules and wisdom.

Now, I suppose, really, that if you looked at this one from a certain light, you would have to call it a 'chick-flick.'

I'm not really sure if I knew that going in, and to tell you the truth, in the first 15 or 20 minutes I was getting a little restless. But then, I don't know what happened, I mean I can't recognize the exact moment it caught me, but at a certain point I felt a tear roll down my cheek and actually land on my jacket and I remember thinking *"Oh, my."*

This one had me, for sure.

It's about young love and it's clean and sweet and nice.

Finally, a picture that was actually moving. There is hope after all.

Now, I want more. What to see next?

I don't know, but I highly recommend Brooklyn.

Point Break

I didn't have the vaguest idea what this was, I just saw part of a preview (it seemed like a good idea at the time), and so while Carol went to see some girlie movie, I chose this one.

Oh, My, God.

If you are a boy, under the age of 17, it's okay for you to see this movie. Anyone else, just stay away.

Let me tell you: It's really a good thing it was dark in that theater, because I was so embarrassed to be there. I am SO glad they turned the lights down. Even though we were in Las Vegas, a thousand miles from home, I still didn't want to risk the chance of anyone seeing me.

There was a thinly disguised plot about some super athletes trying to... Oh, never mind, it doesn't really matter. The whole thing was like a string of magazine covers.

Nothing really made sense, it was all about surfing and skiing and rock climbing and women in bikinis and guys with lots of tattoos.

The most entertaining thing about the whole experience was this young woman sitting to my left, who was texting and looking at facebook the whole time.

She had a lot of interesting friends.

Arrival

Starring Amy Adams, Jeremy Renner, Forest Whitaker

November 18, 2016

Arrival is about the 'arrival' of gigantic spaceships that land in various locations around the globe, and one woman's (that would be Amy Adams, world's foremost linguistics professor) attempts to communicate with them.

The sad part about this movie (not counting the fact that it is the most boring piece of crap ever put on film) is that Amy Adams' character had a baby, raised her, who then died of some horrible disease when she was just a young woman. They showed all of this in a five minute sequence of flashbacks at the start of the film.

Why? Probably to give us something to care about, but that didn't work either, as Amy Adams character is so insipid, so boring, so devoid of emotion, that even her *losing her child* didn't get us to care.

And it certainly didn't matter a whit whether or not she was able to communicate with these outer space bozos.

Of course if she had been able to communicate with them, that is before the friggin movie was 9/10 of the way over, then it could have been more interesting.

Now, when I say *'could have been more interesting'*, what I mean by that is if they substituted everyone in the cast for likeable people, changed the script completely so that it wasn't a vapid, dreary, unbelievable piece of crap, and if they had brightened it up a bit, as opposed to having every scene in fog, shadows and darkness, then it could have been a better movie.

Oh, yes, and lose the friggin haz-mat suits. Jesus! No one wants to see a bunch of geeks walking around in those things.

And while you're rewriting the entire script, please leave out all the parts about spaceships, aliens, space suits, and anything else that has anything to do with trying to communicate with a bunch of extra-terrestrial nincompoops.

Because *NO ONE CARES!*

August: Osage County

Starring Meryl Streep, Juliette Lewis, Sam Shepard, Julia Roberts, Dermot Mulroney, Ewan McGregor, Abigail Breslin

This is a nice little story about a typical American family. That is, a story of a *REALLY SCREWED UP* typical American family. You know, kind of like yours. And mine. Only hopefully yours and mine are not screwed up to the extent that is portrayed in this film. One of the reasons this film is so good is because most of us can relate to the dysfunctionality of many of the characters, at least in some small way. We have all known people just like these. Or at the very least we've seen these traits exhibited in some of our friends, or acquaintances, or even in family members. Or, heaven forbid, in ourselves.

The acting in this movie is superb, on all counts. How this didn't get nominated for best picture is beyond me. Is there a committee that figures out which movies to nominate? Or is it by ballot? In any case, "August: Osage County" *not* being nominated, while "Gravity" is, has got to be a cruel and vicious joke. Or maybe it is just another example of the 'Dumbing Down' of America.

Meryl Streep is over-the-top as a cantankerous and vindictive pill-popping family matriarch and she is brilliant. As is the rest of the cast. Each one of them has delivered a sterling performance. This movie is as real as it gets. Real people in real-life situations that are totally believable. There is not one boring moment. In some ways, it reminded me of "Who's Afraid Of Virginia Woolf," (as in movies about screwed-up people), and a little of "The Celebration" another terrific movie about a screwed-up family.

Juliette Lewis is extraordinary as the flighty and neurotic daughter of Meryl Streep. Julia Roberts plays another daughter, a controlling, angry, emotionless being, and does an excellent job as well.

It's kind of funny, now that I'm thinking back on the movie, that the men's parts in this film, while strong, are actually secondary to the women's roles. Now, that's a switch. But be that as it may, though their roles may be lessor, the men are as good as the women, and the whole cast blends together to form an entirely believable family portrait.

You know, this is billed as a comedy/drama but about halfway through there's nothing more to laugh at because it begins to dawn on us just how unhinged these folks really are.

This one is highly recommended.

The Counselor

Starring
M. Fassbender
B. Pitt
P. Cruz
C. Diaz
J. Bardem

You know, even though this movie got bad reviews, I figured it would be good anyway. I mean it had Cameron Diaz, Brad Pitt, Penelope Cruz, Michael Fassbender. It was directed by Ridley Scott, who is credited with some very fine movies, among them *Alien, Thelma and Louise, Blade Runner,* and *BlackHawk Down,* for gosh sakes!

So how could it be bad?

When we entered the theatre there were about 16 others in attendance. That was our second clue (bad reviews being the first).

Hey, here's a good idea for a believable plot: A dope deal involving a bunch of kilos of marijuana being smuggled in a sewage pumping truck. They put the dope in 55-gallon drums inside a septic sucking truck, then close it up and fill it up with raw sewage. Now there's a real believable plot.

Because no one would ever want to look in there, right? Of course not.

And no customs inspector on any border would venture to ask why you would be driving a shit truck from Mexico into the United States.

Further, no highway patrolman in any state would be suspicious of a truck carrying raw sewage from Mexico. A foul and disgusting sewage truck, mind you, that was made to *look like* a foul and disgusting sewage truck with a couple of foul and disgusting sewage truck drivers coming into the United States from *MEXICO.*

No, people transport raw sewage into the United States from Mexico all the time.

These points are small potatoes, though, compared to the rest of the movie.

First of all, it is as boring a movie as there ever could be. It is *agonizingly* slow.

The acting is terrible! It was as if they were looking over someone's shoulder and reading their lines. Everyone in the entire movie should be embarrassed.

Michael Fassbender and Penelope Cruz are supposed to be madly in love, but the chemistry between them is absolutely hollow and they are both wooden.

These two were not only unbelievable, they were boring! If we gave a rat's ass about any character, that would be different. But they failed miserably in trying to evoke empathy for anyone, save Penelope Cruz who was an innocent bystander.   Everyone else was a sleazebucket of the first degree. And that would be okay as well, but they were BORING sleazebuckets!

We kept waiting for something to happen. Anything. But instead, we got a whole load of pontificating from everyone. And I mean everyone. Every character, major, minor, bit part, or cameo, all had their grandiose, wordy statements. Most of them sounded like some dime-store philosopher turned wino. Soon, it became just plain embarrassing. Everyone had a sermon. And every one of them went on and on and on and on, all of it signifying absolutely nothing.

My goodness, this one made me angry. Those people should be ashamed of themselves.

You know, a lot of times I kid about movies, tease about how crappy they are. It's fun to lambaste. But this one I am not kidding about. It is horrible. This one makes "Gravity" (which I deplored) seem like "Gone With The Wind."

If you decide to go see this movie, I implore you: Read as many reviews as you can (they are all bad), and *believe them!*

And don't go!

Gravity

Starring
Sandra Bullock
George Clooney

There seem to be two camps regarding this movie. Those that loved it and those that hated it. The people who loved it far outnumber them who hated it, it appears.

Guess which camp this reviewer is in.

Oh, you know me like a book.

Listen, they say that in space, no one can hear you scream.

Well they can certainly hear you scream in a movie theater.

It is really too bad that Sandra Bullock and George Clooney were in it, because if it starred someone such as Keir Dullea it might have had a chance.

But Bullock? Clooney? Please.

I will admit that when they were bouncing around outside the spacecraft it got a little hairy. For those of us who fear heights, anyway. I must admit I was squirming in my chair.

But ten minutes of squirming does not a movie make.

And neither does an idiotic woman, who is supposed to be an astronaut, howling like a dog.

God have mercy. She reminded me of someone doing a guest appearance on the Carol Burnett show.

And George Clooney? An astronaut? Spare me. He played this like he was Bing Crosby in some sappy Christmas extravaganza.

Not only that, the dialogue in this movie had to have come from a high school drama composition. I mean, what am I missing here?

I know I'm in the minority, but I like to think it's because I set my standards high.

To borrow a quote from another crappy movie, that would be Forest Gump, *"Stupid is as stupid does..."*

AWAKE

AWAKE: The Autobiography Of A Yogi

Oh, wait a minute, *Autobiography of a Yogi* was the name of the book he wrote.

The name of this movie is AWAKE, the Life of Yogananda.

It's about Paramahansa Yogananda. Yep, *that* Paramahansa. My main man. Or at least he was my main man. Back in the day. You know, in the sixties, when people were first catching on to Eastern thought and new and different ways to find spirituality.

In the sixties, our entire culture was going through many radical changes, and the exploration of Eastern religion, philosophy, and spirituality was only one of them.

But these days, now that Eastern Spirituality is thoroughly ensconced into our culture, his life, and this movie, seem dated. Almost like watching a silent film. An antique, if you will. Back then, when he was fresh and new, and the guru/swami/maharishi game was just catching on, it was very exciting and cool and hip.

Now, it's kind of old hat.

Just like the movie about the pelicans. We see pelicans *all* the time around here. And we love them, do we not? They are fascinating and seeing them is like looking back in time.

But please. A whole movie about them? Sorry. The snore factor set in early on.

Same as Yogananda. It would have been fascinating back in the sixties. Wait, it *was* fascinating back then. But now, it just seems dated. Reminded me of a newsreel from grammar school.

Snore.

WILD TALES

I remember the first time I ever got 'high' from a movie. It was "Little Murders" by Jules Feiffer and it was around 1970.

I've gotten high from movies a few times since then (most notably 'Cowboys And Aliens" from a couple years ago). (hahahaha)

This one made me high, for sure.

But wait. Maybe, just maybe, I was high from the company I was in. Oh yes, absolutely. I went with FIVE (count 'em, five) of my favorite gals! My darling wife Carol, of course, and Karena, Nora, Mimi, and Annalise. What guy wouldn't be high in company like that?

But this was an excellent movie just the same, and it only added to the high.

It's from Argentina, and it is a series of short 'tales.' For once I agree with Mick LaSalle, who said this movie has more emotion, feeling, humor, passion, and fun in the first five minutes than most American movies do in their entirety.

If Mark Twain, or Kurt Vonnegut, or O'Henry or other masters of wit and irony had been movie makers, this is the kind of movie they would have made.

They said that this was the runner-up to the winner of the foreign film awards of 2014. *RUNNER-UP??* If this one came in second, I'd certainly like to see what came in first.

It is excellent in every respect. The camera work, the editing, the stories, the acting... all of it, superb. Exciting, scary, funny, tense, amazing.

One of the reasons we went is because a friend emailed me and said *"Bill, go see 'Wild Tales' at the Rafael. I bet it'll be your favorite movie of the year."*

He was right.

The Walk
Starring Joseph Gordon-Levitt

Hey, afraid of heights? Knees get weak when you're on the side of a precipice? Any acrophobia at all?

Well, then this is the movie for you!

It's about Phillip Petit, the Frenchman who did a tightrope walk between the twin towers in New York City just as the construction of the two buildings was being completed in 1974.

This is a terrific movie, not only because of the height factor, but because it is done so well. Although it is a drama, it is more like a bio-documentary. It is totally believable from start to finish, and it *takes* you, and does not let go until you are white-knuckling it all through the entire actual 'Walk.'

I'm pretty sure that I can't wreck it for you, because it is what it is. A guy doing a tight rope walk between the two highest buildings in the world, and filmed in breathtaking, sweat-inducing, big-screen, technicolor 3-D. Which is not at all necessary, the only reason we saw it in 3-D is because that is all they had when we went.

The view from up there is absolutely spectacular. Many of the shots were taken at sunrise or sunset when the light is at its best, and it was just beautiful.

And then, there was the walk. *"Don't look down,"* I guess is the motto of many a tightrope walker. And that's just fine for them, they don't *have* to look down. But as the movie going audience, WE have to. WE don't have a choice.

And this explains why we were squirming in our seats, white knuckling our arm rests, getting sweaty palms and becoming weak in the knees, and barely stifling the compulsion to get out of our seats and run screaming from the theater.

Hey, you want to be *moved* when you go to a movie, do you not?

This one will definitely move you.

Killer Joe

Starring Matthew McConaughey, Gina Gershon, Thomas Haden Church, Emile Hirsch, Juno Temple

This movie was directed by William Friedkin, who did 'The French Connection' and 'The Excorcist,' among others. So there was promise going in.

It isn't playing in that many theaters, so we had to drive across the bridge to see it. And I'm so glad we did.

Let me tell you right off, that this was one of the best movies I have ever seen.

I'm not one to divulge plots, story lines, or anything else about a movie, especially a great one, such as this. If you want more information, read some other reviews. I will say this, though: it has to do with trailer trash, dope deals and the like, and it is not for the squeamish.

The reason that this one is so great is that it takes you, from the second it comes on the screen, until the final credits start to roll, it takes you, and does not let go for one single moment. The tension builds and builds. Now, some people might say, whoa, Bill, I don't want to be tense in a movie. And I say, well, then, maybe you should just stay home. But the tension, and one of the reasons I liked it so much, is that it is REAL. As in believable.

OH MY GOD.

Matthew McConaughey is brilliant, as is Gina Gershon, as is Thomas Haden Church. Everyone else is brilliant as well. Wow.

Not since 'Reservoir Dogs' have I been this tense in a movie. This one is exciting, and violent, and sexual, and tense, and exciting, and sexual, and violent. And tense. And SO well done. Oh, did I repeat myself?

Well, did I say HOLY SH-T?

Everyone in this movie did an EXCELLENT job with their part. You wanna get taken for a terrific ride?

Go see this one.

OH MY GOD.

The Banshees Of Inisherin

With Colin Farrell, Brendan Gleeson and Kerry Condon

At last! Something new, something original, something fresh, something interesting. Something provocative, touching, funny, well done and heartbreaking.

Thank you, thank you, thank you.

Everyone in the cast was perfect.

Oh, to think I almost missed this. Some people told me this movie was kind of slow, so I put it off.

It was not slow for me.

My goodness, I was riveted from the first moments.

Now, I'm not going to tell you the plot, or divulge the surprises, because that would spoil the fun. But I will say mostly it's about men being men.

Not only is Colin Farrell a great actor, he's worth the price of admission for his eyebrows alone.

I watched it at home through HBO Max. I was very fortunate to have subtitles because the Irish brogues are a little hard to understand.

With the subtitles, I got everything. Thank god.

This one is up for a whole slew of awards and rightfully so. It's the best movie I've seen in quite some time.

I watched it again the following night.

Go see it, or watch it at home, but see it.

Spoilers here:

(I think the whole thing is one huge metaphor for war, and how the males of our species create strife through stubbornness, and righteousness and the need to dominate others. It is built into our gender. That's what we <u>do</u>. The strife between the two guys in this film was just small potatoes but it represented exactly how men relate to one another and how it escalates and leads to bigger things and soon things that can't be forgiven and there is no resolution ever, and it's been that way since the beginning of time and it will never ever change because it is part and parcel of our very nature. If you've got a penis, there's going to be trouble. Period).

I just can't get over how perfect (for me) of a movie that was. Every single thing was spot-on. The lighting, the camera angles, the shots, the landscapes, the clouds, the music, and of course the acting. Each person in the entire movie was perfect for their particular part. The sister's character was brilliant. As were the main protagonists, both of them. The guy who played Dominic — perfect. What a job he did. And his father as well — who got the worst come-uppence anyone could ever get, by losing his son. And the two guys in the bar, Tweedle dum and Tweedledee, who each took turns saying the same sentence … the biddy in the corner store, the old woman soothsayer…. Every single one of them was absolutely fabulous in every way. OMG, the priest, jumping out of the confession box and yelling "YES, YOU

WILL BE FUCKED" at Gleeson's character, Colm. Was that fecking hilarious, or what? The camera angles! The clouds! I'm telling you, for me, this was a flawless work of art. I'm still shaking my head in wonder.

When I say this is a man's movie, I mean that men can relate to it simply because they are men. I could easily identify with both of those guys. A lot of women don't get it. Because they think in feminine terms. Terms like solving problems, nurturing others, things like that. But men need to dominate. It's in our genes. We have a built-in agenda, placed in us by nature to keep the species going.

The children's nursery rhyme actually is more profound in it's description of the different natures of men and women when it says what little girls are made of -- sugar and spice, and everything nice. And shows the same profound accuracy when it comes to boys: Snips and snails and puppy dog's tails.

In other words, guys are shit-disturbers from the get-go. It's in our genes. If you've got a penis, there's gonna be trouble.

To me, the whole thing is one huge metaphor for war, and how the males of our species create strife through stubbornness, and righteousness and the need to dominate. It is built into our gender since the beginning of time. We are animals, after all. So that's what we <u>do</u>. And the strife between the two guys in this film was just small potatoes but it represented exactly how men relate to one another and how it escalates and leads to bigger things and soon things that can't be forgiven and there is no resolution ever.

Which is why the ending was so perfect. Because it will never be resolved until one or both of them are dead. And when they're dead, the next two guys will replace them.

And that's the way it works. That's the way it goes. That's the way it is.

And a lot of us think well, does it really have to be this way, why can't we make a peaceful world, but each one of us (men, that is) still get all caught up in trying to dominate the next guy in one way or another because it is built into our gender and it is never ever going to stop.

I used to think that someday, we'll all evolve to a point of enlightenment and there will be no more fighting, no war, we'll all live in peace and harmony.

But that is a fairy tale that is not going to happen.

Because the nature of man **is what it is,** and it ain't gonna change, ever.

SISU

Starring (nobody we've ever heard of)

About halfway through game six of the Warriors - Kings playoff series, I saw a 15 second commercial for a movie called 'SISU' (rhymes with tissue) which looked a hell of a lot more interesting than what the Dubs were doing (which was getting hammered mercilessly by the Kings).

This was supposed to be a charming little ultra-violent movie about a one-man wrecking machine who kills a bunch of Nazis.

Nazis getting theirs? Right up my alley.

So I forgot about the game (it didn't get any better) and rushed out to take it all in.

Although it had overtones of Quentin Tarantino written all over it, it certainly was no "Inglorious Basterds."

No, this one cuts out most of the fluff (such as a story line) and gets right to the mayhem.

Think Sergio Leone (without the long, drawn-out shots, thank you) meets Robert Rodriguez (from Dusk Till Dawn) only without morphing into Sci-Fi dragons.

Our protagonist is a guy who's prospecting out in Northern Finland as WWII is winding toward it's end. He finds a bunch of gold and packs it up in his saddlebags; he's riding a horse and he has a cute little dog — I guess they wanted to throw a little 'Western' atmosphere into it.... Anyway, he runs across a group of Nazis. Actually a caravan with several trucks and a tank, etc, and even a truck carrying a bunch of obviously kidnapped women who are being used for the fat ugly dirty hairy stinking Nazis sexual pleasures.

We find out later, through a series of titles labeling chapters throughout the movie (ala Quentin Tarantino) that our hero is a former bad-ass killer for some elite group... it doesn't really matter what group, just know that this guy is the combo of every Liam Nissan hero, or every Sylvester Stallone Rambo movie — in other words, you don't want to mess with this guy.

Not only is it impossible to kill him, he can take on entire regiments of fully-armed soldiers with no more than a pocket knife and a cigarette lighter.

Never mind that he's pushing sixty and has arm flaps like Charles Bronson in those old "Death Wish" vigilante flicks.

But one needs to be able to overlook some of these small flaws to enjoy a little gratuitous Nazi killing, doesn't one?

Anyway, he's still as fast as a cat which is proven when he takes on a small herd of Nazis (there were five or six of them all armed to the teeth) and killing all of them. He surprises the first Nazi, who is behind him with an automatic weapon and is ordering him to "Get on your knees", by all of a sudden, in the blink of an eye, driving a huge knife right through his head, temple to temple.

Needless to say, this particular Nazi had a very surprised look on his face.

Now, I know you're not supposed to laugh at these things but I'm sorry. These scenes are SO over the top, and SO ridiculous that they're actually funny.

They next guy he kills in this particular sequence he shoots from under his chin and out of the top of the guys head shoots a geyser of blood like an over-amped fountain.

I had to stifle my laughter because I didn't want the other patrons to think I was some kind of psycho. But I'm telling you, it was hilarious.

There are several more very satisfying scenes of Nazi-slaughtering throughout the movie. And all the ways our protagonist escapes death border on ludicrous — wait, there's no border here, they are one hundred percent ludicrous, each one more ridiculous than the previous.

But as I said, if you want to enjoy seeing Nazis get slaughtered, you have to suspend your belief system for a few minutes.

Obviously, this movie isn't for everyone. But for those of you whom it is, you know who you are.

www.ingramcontent.com/pod-product-compliance
Lightning Source LLC
Chambersburg PA
CBHW051745250726

48659CB00001B/249